PUTTING GOD SECOND

PUTTING GOD SECOND

HOW TO SAVE RELIGION FROM ITSELF

_____

Rabbi Donniel Hartman

BEACON PRESS
BOSTON

BEACON PRESS
Boston, Massachusetts
www.beacon.org

Beacon Press books
are published under the auspices of
the Unitarian Universalist Association of Congregations.

20 19 18 17   8 7 6 5 4 3 2 1

This book is printed on acid-free paper that meets the uncoated paper
ANSI/NISO specifications for permanence as revised in 1992.

Text design and composition by Kim Arney

Library of Congress Cataloging-in-Publication Data

Names: Hartman, Donniel.
Title: Putting God second : how to save religion from itself / Donniel
    Hartman.
Description: Boston : Beacon Press, 2016. | Includes bibliographical
    references and index.
Identifiers: LCCN 2015025755 |
    ISBN 9780807063347 (pbk. : alk. paper) |
    ISBN 9780807053935 (ebook)
Subjects: LCSH: Psychology, Religious. | Abrahamic religions. |
    Apologetics. | Judaism—Apologetic works. | Islam—Apologetics works.
Classification: LCC BL53 .H37 2016 | DDC 200.1/9—dc23 LC record
    available at http://lccn.loc.gov/2015025755

FOR

Michal, Yitzchak, and Talya
A token of my love
A sign of my respect
A prayer that you continue
to find your own religious paths

Rav Huna said in the name
of Rabbi Hiyya bar Aba: "They deserted Me
and did not keep My instructions. (Jeremiah 16:11)
If only they had deserted Me but kept My instructions."

—Midrash Eikhah Rabbah Ptikha 2

CONTENTS

ACKNOWLEDGMENTS

WRITING A BOOK is a deeply personal journey into the depths of one's thoughts, feelings, and words. One of the greatest blessings in my life is that I get to engage in this journey in the company of others who love, support, critique, and inspire me every day. It is a special blessing to be able to thank and acknowledge their role in my life and contribution to this book.

First and foremost my family: my wife, Adina; my children and children-in-law Michal, Noam, Yitzchak, Avital, and Talya; and grandchildren Mia and Sofia. Adina, for whom God can only be first, who keeps God and religion alive in the consciousness of our family. I fight from the inside because of you. My children, to whom this book is dedicated, who are always in my mind and heart, and who are the most significant audience and religious partners I have. The love and care that engulfs our lives is the source of my strength and inspiration. My grandchildren and their gift of infinite joy and love, who energize and fill me every day, and whose world this book hopes to change. My mother, Bobbie, and my father, David z"l, my first and most significant teachers and my greatest supporters. The joy of seeing this book in print is diminished by my Abba's death, for though he so much wanted to see it at this stage, it was not to be.

This book was written in the company of a unique community of scholars, teachers, supporters, and students at the Shalom Hartman Institute, where I have been blessed to learn and work over the last thirty years. To the friends and supporters of the institute who provide the foundation and backing every day to enable this remarkable enterprise to thrive, and for the gift to be able to lead it. To my colleagues, individuals of great intellect and kind hearts, who generously give of their time and efforts to challenge, assist, teach, and advise. To think, create, work, and dream in your presence is a gift beyond measure. In particular, I want to thank Avi Sagi, who always makes time to talk, advise, and carefully read and critique everything I write, and Yitzhak Benbaji and Noam Zion for their significant input.

To my students and friends at the institute in Israel and North America, who accompanied me and the ideas of this book over the last ten years, whose religious lives and probing questions shaped every page, and who shared the passion and need to engage in saving religion from itself.

To Bishop Peter Eaton and Imam Abdullah Antepli, who provided critical advice and assistance and encouraged me to write for religious people at large. To David Schnell, who read the first draft and whose "layperson's" perspective was invaluable. To Or Rose, who offered a hand of friendship at a critical time. To the wonderful people at Beacon Press and in particular Amy Caldwell, who embraced the book and nurtured it with professionalism and love.

And finally, to my editor, Charlie Buckholtz, who turned the ideas into beautiful words and sentences, and who served as my primary *hevrutah* for every argument, indeed every word. One yearns to be clear and one writes to be heard. Without Charlie, this book would have been neither.

———

RELIGION'S AUTOIMMUNE DISEASE

MY BROTHER-IN-LAW WAS killed in the Lebanon War of 1982. Every Memorial Day, for over three decades, my family goes to the Israeli national military cemetery where he is interred. The ceremony is the same every year: it commences with a two-minute siren sounded throughout the country, as everyone—in homes, in grocery stores, on the sidewalk, on the highways—literally stops and stands in silent attention. At the military cemetery, kaddish, the mourner's prayer, is then recited by a family member of one of the fallen; a government representative speaks on behalf of the country; rifles are discharged in a military salute; a trumpet plays a funeral dirge; and a military chaplain offers a traditional Jewish prayer for the dead. The ceremony is simple, solemn, mournful, and raw.

But every year the chaplain recites one line that unsettles me. As he chants the request that God on High will bestow an everlasting peace and rest on my brother-in-law, and all others who died in the service of protecting our country, the fallen are designated as having died "al kiddush Hashem"—in the sanctification of God's name. My brother-in-law was a decorated hero who endangered his life daily as a deputy squadron commander in the Israeli Air Force. The State of Israel can never repay the debt that it owes him for his contribution to our survival. But what do God and the sanctification of God's name have to do with fighting for our country—let alone his death? His plane was shot down by a Syrian surface-to-air missile over the Beka Valley. He was fighting in a war that Israeli society came to condemn. Ultimately, the Lebanon war was judged as having violated our strict principles of limiting the use of the Israel Defense Forces to wars of self-defense—and not the establishment of a new political order in a neighboring state, as was the case in the first Lebanon War.

Soldiers are required to be willing to offer the ultimate sacrifice, without the benefit of historical hindsight. My brother-in-law in the sky, myself as a tank commander on the ground, and tens of thousands of others thought we were fighting to protect our northern borders from terrorist infiltrators. Our inability to know at the time that the war far exceeded this just cause belittles neither the heroism nor the enormity of the sacrifice. Historical hindsight does teach us, however, that my brother-in-law's death was probably not necessary for the security of Israel. It was certainly not necessary for the sanctity of God's name.

Why is there an intrinsic association between the wars we fight and the will of God? Between protecting Israel and the sanctification of God's name? It could be that this association is made as a comfort to those left behind. Framing my brother-in-law's death as an act of sanctification, which in turn secures salvation after death "under the wings of God," ennobles it with an aura of not only physical but also spiritual heroism.

I wonder, however, if the comfort offered to those mourning the fallen may be outweighed by a potentially greater consequence—not to the soul of my brother-in-law but to the soul of Israel. When we invoke God as our partner in politics, we identify our will and interests as inherently shared by God. But are they necessarily the same? When God is conflated with country, does it serve the moral and spiritual aspirations of Israel—or undermine them? Does it challenge Israel to live up to divine standards, or does it co-opt God into the service of human political institutions? In this framework, is God a force for good—for challenging, prodding, critiquing, and correcting national interests and policies—or does the divine stamp of approval provide religious cover for immoral acts motivated by self-interest?

When our wars are uniformly sanctified, and our fallen soldiers are memorialized as religious martyrs at official state ceremonies, I worry that the reality may be the latter.

THE RETURN OF GOD

Over three thousand years ago, the fertile basin of the Middle East gave birth to a new idea that altered human and religious history. The idea was of one God, creator of the world, who is both singular in number and unique in quality; who is independent, self-sufficient, and transcendent, but at the same time profoundly interested in and concerned for the world and humanity; who is loving and forgiving, as well as judging and wrathful; who commands and challenges humanity to be loyal and faithful to the divine and compassionate and just with our fellow human beings.

This idea in turn gave rise over the millennia to Judaism, Christianity, and Islam, and their countless denominations and affiliations, each with a distinct take on how life with the one God should be lived. As these religions entered the world stage, alongside their charge to love God and love humanity, they began to wage war with those who preceded or followed them. Wherever monotheism developed, it was accompanied by the belief that the one God could be truly represented or correctly understood by only one faith community. Love of God, or more accurately being loved by God, was perceived to be a zero-sum game—the more one was loved, the less another could be.

And so, together with the love of neighbor came the hatred of the other. Together with kindness to those in need came the murder of those who disagreed. Monotheism became a mixed blessing and a double-edged sword.

Why have monotheistic religions produced such a checkered past? More important, what type of future do they have in store for us? These questions are particularly pressing since the last two decades have seen religion—particularly the monotheistic Abrahamic faiths of Judaism, Christianity, and Islam—emerge from the twentieth-century quasi-hibernation imposed on it by a coalition of secular nationalism, fascism, communism, and liberal democracy. In this time, we have seen religion arise as a central force in world politics and frequent instigator of global conflict.

The majority of the great conflicts and conflagrations of the twentieth century were clashes of a predominantly national and secular political nature. In the last decade of the twentieth century, however, this geopolitical picture began to shift. We witnessed the first stirrings of what would become the multiple manifestations of global Islamic terror, as the Middle East, Africa, and Asia became sites of pitched battles both within Islam and between Christianity and Islam. Semisecular dictators have been replaced by Islamic parties, and Muslim and Jewish religious ideologies are increasingly mainstreamed into political governance in ways that tend to fuel and exacerbate conflicts. Europe has become a frontline in the struggle between secular nationalism and Islam. In the United States, religion is playing an increasingly influential and often contentious role in political discourse and public policy.

It is no understatement to say that the last two decades have been painting the twenty-first century in strongly religious hues.

THE "GOD DELUSION" DELUSION: FAITH AND ITS CONSEQUENCES

The reemergence of God as a dominant force in world affairs, shaping both the fates of nations and the daily existence of ordinary individuals, poses fundamental questions about the role of religion in human life. One of the most significant of these, and the one that guides this book, is this: What does faith in God do to a person? That is, when God enters the conversation and dictates human ethical and social norms, is it a force for good or evil? For action or complacency? For moral progress or moral corruption?

To ask what faith in God does to a person is not the same as asking what faith in God gives to a person. This second question holds different answers for different types of religious personalities. For the spiritually attuned, the mere experience of God's presence can fill one's life with joy, awe, and love. For the more average person of faith, the religious "folk," faith in God offers access, if not a substantive claim, to God's power and grace, guidance and forgiveness, in this world and perhaps in the next. Both groups share a clear and profound intuition that something is fundamentally flawed in the notion of a world without God. For the spiritually attuned, it is the flatness of a life without transcendence. For ordinary religious believers, it is the emptiness of a life without hope for order, and the crushing sense of helplessness in confronting the daily challenges of pain and chaos without recourse to a transcendent source of power and agency. Those whose lives entail many journeys through the "valley of the shadow of death" quite understandably prefer to "fear no harm, for you are with me" (Psalm 23:4), rather than to tread such treacherous paths unguided, unprotected, and alone.

For the person of faith, to believe is most often not a decision but an outcome of the search to fill a void that is experienced with palpable immediacy in everyday life. As a result, this faith is by and large impervious to critical analysis and counterclaims. The human species may or may not be under the spell of "the God delusion," as Richard Dawkins claims, and Christopher Hitchens may or may not have been right that "God is not great." The fact remains that no argument for either of these propositions will be likely to move the person of faith. For the spiritually attuned, the reality and intensity of the religious experience is its own self-validating confirmation. For the average believer, a deep existential need makes faithlessness unimaginable. As Clifford Geertz rightfully posits in *The Interpretation of Cultures*, chaos does not undermine faith in God; rather, chaos makes faith in God necessary. Even after the Enlightenment and the Holocaust, the number of atheists in foxholes hovers steadily near zero.

My concern with the question of what faith in God does to a person is not meant to question the validity of faith nor undermine the legitimacy of the enterprise. Rather, it is meant to be an internal exploration of the practical and conceptual consequences of faith. The questions of whether God exists or is merely a human fabrication, of whether or what we ought to believe, already fill countless volumes, and belong to a different conversation from those that I explore in this book. I am more interested in examining how our beliefs, and the life path faith sets us on, affect our identities—the way we see ourselves and others, and the way we treat people. How does faith change us? Does it make us better people—kinder, gentler and more compassionate to others? Does it alter our perspective on things like violence, war, and suffering?

In light of religion's resurgence as a significant power in shaping the world, it is critical that the faithful take an honest look at the types of people and communities our systems are producing and evaluate the results according to our own self-described values and aspirations. The broad geopolitical and socioeconomic impact of religion in the world today demands that people of faith take ownership over the consequences of their ideologies.

"WHO ASKED THIS OF YOU?": RELIGION'S NOBLE FAILURE

Based on some of the most oft-quoted verses in monotheistic scriptures—their "greatest hits," if you will—it might seem surprising that religion could be anything other than an ennobling force in human life. One common feature of all the monotheistic traditions is that their God aspires to create kind, gentle, and compassionate people. Faith in God is not meant merely to inspire one to worship but to change those who worship, and to be a force for generating care and concern for all of God's creatures, in particular those over whom one holds power. Here are a few prominent examples:

> "You shall not wrong a stranger or oppress him, for you were strangers in the land of Egypt. You shall not ill-treat any widow or orphan. If you do mistreat them, I will heed their outcry as soon as they cry out to Me, and My anger shall blaze forth." (Exodus 22:20–23)

> "Hear this, you who trample the needy and do away with the poor of the land, saying, 'When will the New Moon be over that we may sell grain, and the Sabbath be ended that we may market wheat?'—skimping on the measure, boosting the price and cheating with dishonest scales, buying the poor with silver and the needy for a pair of sandals, selling even the sweepings with the wheat. The Lord has sworn by himself, the Pride of Jacob: 'I will never forget anything they have done.'" (Amos 8:4–7)

> "You have heard that it was said to the people long ago, 'You shall not murder, and anyone who murders will be subject to judgment.' But I tell you that anyone who is angry with a brother or sister will be subject to judgment. Again, anyone who says to a brother or sister, '*Raca*,' ["You worthless one!"] is answerable to the Sanhedrin [court]. And anyone who says, 'You fool!' will be in danger of the fire of hell. Therefore, if you are offering your gift at the altar and there remember that your brother or sister has something against you, leave your gift there in front of the altar. First

go and be reconciled to them; then come and offer your gift."
(Matthew 5:21–25)

"Then the King will say to those on his right, 'Come, you
who are blessed by my Father; take your inheritance, the
kingdom prepared for you since the creation of the world.
For I was hungry and you gave me something to eat, I was
thirsty and you gave me something to drink, I was a stranger
and you invited me in, I needed clothes and you clothed me,
I was sick and you looked after me, I was in prison and you
came to visit me. Then the righteous will answer him, 'Lord,
when did we see you hungry and feed you, or thirsty and give
you something to drink? When did we see you a stranger and
invite you in, or needing clothes and clothe you? When did
we see you sick or in prison and go to visit you?' The King
will reply, 'Truly I tell you, whatever you did for one of the
least of these brothers and sisters of mine, you did for me.'"
(Matthew 25:34–40)

"It is not righteousness that you turn your faces towards the
East or West (in prayer). But it is righteousness to believe in
Allah and the Last Day and the Book and the Messengers. To
spend of your substance out of love for Him, for your kin,
for orphans, for the needy, for the wayfarer, for those who
ask, and for the ransom of slaves." (Quran 2:177)

"Abu Huraira reported that Allah's Messenger (May peace
be upon him) said: One who makes efforts (for his earnings
to be spent) on a widow and the destitute is like a striver in
the cause of Allah, and I think he also said: He is like one
who constantly stands for prayer and observes fast without
breaking it." (Sahih Muslim 42:7107)

Against the backdrop of these sources, and thousands of
similar others, the failure of religion to produce individuals

and societies that champion the values advocated in them is both puzzling and deeply unsettling. Even more troubling is that often religious faith itself is the catalyst that emboldens individuals and governments to murder, maim, harm, and control others in the service of "their" God. While it is not credible to suggest that people of faith are definitively worse than those who do not believe, the fact that a life with God does not seem consistently to make people better is a failure of religion on its own terms, and ought to be a source of consternation for any serious believer.

This problem is not new, nor does it reflect an outsider's critique of religion. In fact, it has hovered around monotheistic traditions since their inception, formulated and addressed by the very first carriers of the one God's word, the biblical prophets:

> Cry with full throat, without restraint, raise your voice like a horn and declare unto My people their transgression, and to the house of Jacob their sins. Yet they seek Me daily, eager to learn My ways, as a nation that did righteousness and forsook not the ordinance of their God, they ask of Me righteous ordinances, they delight in drawing near to God. "Why have we fasted, and yet You do not see? Why have we afflicted our soul, and You pay no attention?" Behold, in the day of your fast you pursue your business, and perform all your labors. Behold, you fast for strife and contention, and to smite with the fist of wickedness. You fast not this day so as to make your voice to be heard on high; is this the fast I desire? The day for a man to afflict his soul? Is it to bow down his head as a bulrush, and to spread sackcloth and ashes under him? Will you call this a fast, and an acceptable day to the Lord? Is not this the fast that I have chosen: to loosen the fetters of wickedness, to undo the bands of the yoke, and to let the oppressed go free, and that you break every yoke? Is it not to distribute your bread to the hungry, and bring the poor that

are cast out to your house? When you see the naked, that you cover him, and that thou hide not yourself from your own flesh? (Isaiah 58:1–7)

Isaiah's admonitions evoke a rare moment in Jewish antiquity. Idolatry is the prevalent deviance of the biblical era, culminating in divine rejection and the Babylonian Exile. Indeed, for most of biblical history Jews rejected God and opted for idolatry. The Bible can be effectively summarized as the history of a Creator yearning to create a holy people who seek the divine and commit themselves to walking in its ways, but who regularly choose instead to ignore it and walk in the way of the idolatrous Ba'al. Isaiah, however, addresses a scenario in which people actually seem to be turning to God, expressing the desire for relationship through ritual devotion.

At first glance, this ought to be one of the great moments in the Bible. At long last, the Jewish people and God are on the same page: "They seek me daily, eager to learn my ways." Is this not precisely the thing for which God has so long yearned? Yet it is at this very moment of rigorous ritual commitment that God must angrily intervene to let them know they have fallen far astray from the path; that they are lost. God tells them, in essence, that while claiming to be a people who want to follow the divine path, they have abandoned it by ignoring their moral responsibility to others. "Did you not hear Me," God asks through the prophets, again and again. "There is something else that I want from you?"

Hear the words of the Lord, you chieftains of Sodom. Give ear to your gods' instructions, you folk of Gomorrah. What need have I of all your sacrifices? I am sated with burnt offerings of rams and suet of fatling and bloods of bulls. I have no delight in lambs and he-goats. That you come to appear before me, who asked this of you? Trample my courts no more. Bringing oblations is futile. Incense is offensive to me. New moon and Sabbath, proclaiming of solemnities, assemblies with inequity, I cannot abide. Your new moons and fixed seasons fill me with loathing. They have become a burden to me. I cannot endure them. And when you lift up your hands, I will turn my eyes away from you. Though you pray at length, I will not listen. Why? Because your hands are stained with crime. Wash yourselves clean. Put your evildoings away from my sight. Cease to do evil. Learn to do good. Devote yourselves to justice. Aid the wrong. Uphold the rights of the orphan. Defend the cause of the widow. (Isaiah 1:10–17)

The people are eager for intimacy with God through the offering of sacrifices. They finally show up with passionate ritual devotion, and God's response, in essence, is to say, Go away! Why is it that your religious life is completely defined by ritual, by devotion to me, to the exclusion of everything I said about how to treat others? Why are you ignoring the other part of what I have commanded?

Why does a life with God—a God who so clearly commands "Love your neighbor as yourself, I am the Lord your God" (Leviticus 19:18)—so consistently fail to achieve its own stated goals?

ASSIGNING BLAME: "THE DEVIL QUOTES SCRIPTURE"

Advocates of religion tend to answer this question by ascribing religious failure exclusively to human weakness and ignorance. It is not a consequence of faith or tradition but of a flawed humanity consumed by a form of original sin. Contrary to the gospel of Woody Allen, who posited in his film *Love and Death* that God is an underachiever, defenders of the Almighty counter that people are the real underachievers, incapable of true commitment to perfect divine directives and to meeting the obligations that, if only followed correctly, would remake them, their families, and their communities. The Bible echoes this tradition when describing humanity in the aftermath of the Flood: "And the Lord said to Himself: Never again will I doom the earth because of man, since the devisings of man's mind are evil from his youth." (Genesis 8:21)

God may charge us with a mission, to live a life of righteousness and justice . . . but the flesh is weak, and the bar perhaps unrealistically high. From this perspective, God is a romantic, perennially yearning for us to reach for standards of moral sensitivity that will require us to open our eyes and respond to the suffering surrounding us, but we cannot seem to muster the inner fortitude required to live up to those aspirations.

Conversely, religion's critics locate the primary blame for the moral failure of religious people in religion itself. For them, this failure is not the consequence of ignoring the divine command but of fulfilling it. For such critics, religion itself is the original sin that "poisons everything," as per Christopher Hitchens in *God Is Not Great*. They argue that surrounding the scriptures' advocacy of moral sensitivity and compassion are a multitude of sources commanding holy war, religious discrimination and persecution, and triumphalism, to say nothing of gender inequality, racism, and homophobia. These, they claim, are in fact the dominant themes of these traditions, far outweighing the others, and history seems to bear this reading out. It is no wonder, they argue, that religion has been the driving force behind so much bloodshed and oppression.

When the advocates of religion, on the one hand, and critics of God, on the other, make their claims and counterclaims, it is evident that they are reading completely different books. Confronting morally difficult or disturbing texts, advocates tend to rationalize, apologize, minimize, reinterpret, or otherwise divert attention away from them. Conversely, critics who claim that religion is inherently corrupt and corrupting either ignore these traditions' powerful moral insights or marginalize them as insignificant, clearly outweighed by contradictory imperatives.

The interpretive moves of the advocates help to assuage the cognitive dissonance of the enlightened believer, but they do nothing to relieve the profound impact these texts have on the great many others who take their messages at face value. As Shakespeare sharply observed, "The devil can cite Scripture for his purpose," and it is important to emphasize that the devil does not misquote scripture. He has no need, for the tradition provides him with all the ammunition he requires. Where religion serves to fuel injustice, it comes armed with chapter and verse.

On the other hand, the claims of the critics ignore the experienced reality of religious people, for whom these verses that enshrine positive ethics and values are a central, driving component of their religious consciousness, prompting intense moral striving and achievement. To trivialize or gloss over them is to overlook the positive impact that religion has on the lives of countless people and communities, inspiring and compelling them to compassion, charity, justice, and good deeds. The picture, ultimately, is more complex than either side tends to recognize.

RELIGION'S AUTOIMMUNE DISEASE

The truth is that monotheistic religion is neither perfectly good—and thus its failures the exclusive result of human weakness—nor perfectly evil, poisoning the character of all who adopt it with a crippling spiritual disease. The central argument of this book is that religion's (and religions') spotty moral track record cannot be written off to either a core corruption in human nature or an inherently corrupt scripture. Rather it is my contention that a life of faith, while obligating moral sensitivity, also very often activates a critical flaw that supports and encourages immoral impulses. These impulses, given free rein to flourish under the cloak of religious piety, undermine the ultimate moral agendas of religions and the types of communities and societies they aspire to build. The argument of this book is that this critical flaw, when recognized, can be overcome.

This frequently overlooked phenomenon that accounts for the moral underachievement of our monotheistic traditions is what I term religion's "autoimmune disease"—a disease in which the body's immune system, which is designed to fight off external threats, instead attacks and destroys the body's own healthy cells and tissues. This diagnosis is meant to help conceptualize the dynamics through which religions so often undermine their own deepest values and attack their professed goals. While God obligates the good and calls us into its service, God simultaneously and inadvertently makes us morally blind.

The nature of monotheism's autoimmune disease is that God's presence, and the human religious desire to live in relationship with God, often distracts religion's adherents from their traditions' core moral truths. Such a presence can so consume our field of vision that we see nothing other than God (a recipe for ethical bankruptcy); can lead to claims of *chosenness* that encourage self-aggrandizing reflexivity (transforming us into people who see only ourselves); or can cause us to see scripture as morally perfect, despite the failures embedded within it (thereby sanctifying the morally profane).

Ultimately, I believe that religion's record of moral mediocrity will persist as long as communities of faith fail to recognize the ways in which our faith itself is working against us. In other words, only when we are able to discern, within ourselves and our traditions, the symptoms of religion's autoimmune diseases, will we be able to begin developing remedies that enable religion to heal itself and reclaim its noble aspirations.

JUDAISM: A MODEL PATIENT

If religion is not all bad, where does it go wrong? What aspects of its moral core have shown themselves to be particularly vulnerable to being co-opted and corrupted? Where are the weak links, the permeable walls in the cell structure of its immune system that leave it exposed to infection and breakdown?

This book is an attempt to answer these questions through a sustained analysis of monotheism's autoimmune diseases as expressed in the Jewish tradition, and a prescription for how they can be overcome. Though incidences of these conditions are found throughout the other monotheistic faiths, it must be left to the religious leaders of these communities to diagnose the sources and symptoms in all their cultural specificity and to suggest potential treatments and cures that remain embedded in their traditional narratives. Judaism here is meant to serve as both a salient paradigm for this shared challenge and a template for how the challenge might be conceptualized and addressed by those of other faiths.

In using Judaism as my "model patient," I will not be positing all-inclusive arguments or conclusions about the Jewish tradition in general or attempting to exhaust the totality of Judaism's discourse on these issues. Rather, I will selectively highlight sources that show how and where Judaism, as a monotheistic faith, has been susceptible to infection by these autoimmune diseases. My point in doing so is both to explain a central dynamic within Judaism and to use Judaism to make the point of how monotheism can attack and undermine its own goals. Similarly, in modeling how religion can overcome these diseases, I will use certain ideas within the Jewish tradition to create what I hope is a compelling narrative of how religion can heal itself from itself. My argument is that the core features of this narrative are deeply rooted within Judaism itself.

That said, my choice of Judaism as a case study does not stem merely from proficiency therein, nor from my belief that traditions are best critiqued by their insiders. I choose Judaism because as a member of this faith, I have a personal investment in exposing its shortcomings for the sake of attempting to heal them—offering a narrative of what my tradition can and ought to stand for. In truth, I am trying to save my own religion from itself.

This need for healing is particularly acute with the rebirth of Israel and the return of the Jewish people to sovereignty and power. Now, after two thousand years, Jews, like Christians and Muslims for centuries now, must come to terms with the impact of their faith on their surroundings. We are often self-congratulatory about our record of tolerance and compassion toward others, pointing to two millennia of diaspora life, and our support for religious freedom and coexistence. For much of this history, however, we were a powerless people—and a powerless people is always a moral one, as self-interest positions one on the side of the downtrodden.

Now, however, we find ourselves in a dramatically different reality and a much improved condition. We not only have the ability to protect ourselves but also the power to harm others. As the short history of Israel has revealed, it is all too often the same people who speak in the name of religion who come down on the side of discrimination toward the non-Jewish national minorities in Israel; who are comfortable wielding political power to limit religious freedom for non-Jews; for whom all wars that Israel wages are by definition just and ought to be supported; and who campaign most vociferously against pursuing peace with our Palestinian neighbors.

Judaism is my patient because, as a rabbi and teacher, I am engaged every day in a struggle for its soul, as I seek to ensure that Judaism in Israel is a force for good.

CHAPTER OUTLINE

Chapter 1 explores the nature of Judaism's commitment to creating a human being of high moral standards, how that ethical impulse is framed and why this framing is particularly vulnerable to faith's autoimmune disease. The second chapter explores two primary and distinct manifestations of religion's autoimmune diseases, which I coin God Intoxication and God Manipulation. Chapters 3 and 4 suggest conceptual approaches, deeply enshrined within traditional values and narratives, to treating and preventing these autoimmune conditions and that free the life of faith to fulfill its own potentialities and passionate aspirations. Chapter 5 explores where scripture itself, and not its "misinterpreters," goes morally astray, and the implications this has on the meaning of sacred scripture and how a morally centered religious life ought to use it. In chapter 6, I raise the seemingly heretical question, if God is second, whether faith is necessary at all to be a person of religious excellence, a "good Jew." In the conclusion, I explore the relationship between "putting God second" and the central religious value of humility. I argue that God's relationship to creation requires of humanity a more complex sense of self, and that precisely by embracing this complexity we can marshal the religious passion to overcome religion's autoimmune diseases.

Religious scriptures evoke both the sublime heights of human aspiration and the depths of narcissistic moral blindness. The debate over which of these represents "true religion" will always end in bitter stalemate, with both sides holding tightly to the blinkered triumphalism justified by their selective reading of religious scriptures and traditions. My aim in this book is to transcend this futile debate and offer an analysis of religion's failings, as well as provide a resource for its repair. In the final analysis, it is up to the heirs of a religious tradition, in every generation, to decide which sources will inform our religious consciousness and sensibilities. It is up to the advocates and adherents of God's word to assess honestly whether religion is achieving its own core objectives, and if not, to set it fearlessly on a path toward correction.

CHAPTER ONE

YOU ARE YOUR BROTHER'S KEEPER: THE RELIGIOUS ETHIC OF NONINDIFFERENCE

*For I have singled him [Abraham] out, so that he may
instruct his children and his posterity to keep the way
of the Lord by doing what is just and right, in order
that the Lord may bring about for Abraham what
the Lord has promised him. (Genesis 18:19)*

ABRAHAM'S WAY

A teacher of mine used to love to tell the story of a famous Hassidic master who was walking along a cobbled street in Eastern Europe some two hundred years ago, when he heard the cry of a baby coming from his student's house—a cry that pierced the night. He rushed into the house and saw his student enraptured in prayer, swaying in pious devotion. The rabbi walked over to the baby, took her into his arms, sat down, and rocked her to sleep. When the student emerged from his prayers, he was shocked and embarrassed to find his master in his house, holding his baby. "Master," he said, "what are you doing? Why are you here?" "I was walking in the street when I heard crying," he responded, "so I followed it and found her alone." "Master," the student replied, "I was so engrossed in my prayers that I did not hear her." The master replied, "My dear student, if praying

19

makes one deaf to the cries of a child, there is something flawed in the prayer."

The Hassidic master's critique of his student reflects a core commitment of Jewish tradition to the centrality of the ethical—put simply, seeing and responding to the needs of others—that is too often lost in a haze of presumptive piety. Indeed, the centrality of the ethical to Jewish tradition is established at the outset of the story of the first Jew. Offered as the reason underlying Abraham's selection for a special relationship with God—his mission to do "what is just and right"—the Bible locates ethical behavior as the cornerstone of Jewish religious life. But what is the content of this calling? This chapter will explore one of Judaism's central answers to this question: the obligation to "not remain indifferent" (Deuteronomy 22:3), to see the needs of others and to implicate oneself as a part of the solution. In so doing, the chapter provides the critical background for understanding the susceptibility of Judaism's ethical core to the autoimmune disease of monotheistic religious faith.

The narrative context for this chapter's epigraph is a moment of divine self-reflection in which God decides to share the divinely ordained plan for the city of Sodom with God's chosen covenantal partner. The election of Abraham is founded on the understanding that to walk in "the way of the Lord" is to do the "just and right." It is almost as if God communicates Sodom's imminent demise as an object lesson in how these values are to be practiced.

Abraham's response—his impassioned argument calling upon God to live up to the divine essence of justice—"Far be it from You! Shall not the Judge of all the earth deal justly?" (Genesis 18:25)—so often dominates the reading of this story that a key underlying feature is largely forgotten: that Abraham refused to remain indifferent and consequently saw himself as responsible and compelled to intervene on Sodom's behalf. Abraham had every justification in the world simply to look the other way. These were not his people: What business is it of mine? They were part of a depraved and corrupted culture: Maybe they deserve it after all? Moreover, the ruling on their punishment was the revealed judgment of God: Who am I to know better than God? The judge of the earth will certainly deal justly!

However, rather than absolving himself with a Cain-like ethic of "Am I my brother's keeper?" (Genesis 4:9), Abraham chooses the path of responsibility and positions himself as the defender of Sodom. When confronted by injustice, he follows an ethic of nonindifference and in so doing provides a model for what it means to "keep the way of the Lord by doing what is just and right."

DOWN BY THE WELL: FOLLOWING ABRAHAM'S PATH

The most prominent of biblical matriarchs, Rebecca, and the greatest of Jewish leaders, Moses, are each singled out for this very trait. At critical junctures, both faced situations in which they could either be indifferent or choose to see and respond, a test of character that subsequently serves as a turning point in their lives, if not a cornerstone of the favor they find in God's eyes.

In both instances, these pivotal moments occur by a well, which in the Bible is a microcosm of the public sphere, a place of meeting for both locals and travelers. Owned by no one individually, shared by all, the well is designated to serve everyone's most basic needs, friend and stranger alike. However, precisely because it falls within the public domain, it is susceptible to abuse by those with power, making it a hotspot for local politics and struggles, for self-aggrandizement, disenfranchisement, and abuse. In the biblical well narratives, ancient Israelite heroes meet others who have come to fill their basic material needs, and in the process find themselves in need of kindness, protection, or both.

Rebecca is deemed to be of special moral character and a fitting wife for Isaac, by virtue of her care for a stranger in need (in this case, Eliezer, Abraham's emissary). "'Drink, my lord,' she said, and she quickly lowered her jar upon her hand, and let him drink. When she had let him drink his fill, she said, 'I will also draw for your camels, until they finish drinking.' Quickly emptying her jar into the trough, she ran back to the well to draw, and she drew for all his camels." (Genesis 24:18–20) Eliezer, on a mission to find a wife for Isaac, set the criteria for a prospective bride as follows: "Let the maiden to whom I say, 'Please, lower your jar that I may drink,' and who replies, 'Drink, and I will also water your camels'—let her be the one whom You have decreed for Your servant Isaac." (Genesis 28:14) Eliezer, a stranger in a strange land, implicitly poses the question, who is going to see me the way Abraham chose to see Sodom?

Moses does the same, coming to the aid of a group of women being pushed away from the well by male shepherds who were preventing them from feeding their flocks. When he travels to Midian as a lone stranger—one of the most precarious positions of antiquity, making him fair game for all manner of harassment—Moses chooses to involve himself in the affairs of vulnerable strangers. "The priest of Midian had seven daughters, and they came and drew water, and filled the troughs to water their father's flock. And the shepherds came and drove them away; but Moses stood up and helped them, and watered their flock." (Exodus 2:16–17) Rather than minding his own business and exercising understandable caution to protect his own precarious status as stranger, he chose to see the injustice around him, rejecting the safer path of indifference, and to stand with those being wronged.

THE PATH OF MOSES

The quality he displays at the well is the defining characteristic of Moses's life and leadership. We must recall that Moses grows up in the palace of Pharaoh, wanting for nothing, a free and powerful man ensconced in the only home he has ever known.

Why is this person—a man in no obvious need of redemption, totally at home in Egyptian culture—chosen by God to become the leader of the Jewish people? What quality does he embody that merits him to give them the Torah and to become, alongside Abraham, the most significant figure in Jewish history? The answer is that, like Abraham, he is quintessentially a person who takes responsibility for the protection and well-being of others.

Moses's character is established by the Bible the moment he is introduced as an adult. Despite being accepted as a privileged Egyptian, he is characterized as the type of person who chooses not to remain in the insulated and protected environment of Pharaoh's palace but to go out and be among his kin; notwithstanding the fact that to embrace his Jewish identity was in severe contradiction to his self-interest. "Sometime after that, when Moses had grown up, he went out to his kinfolk and saw them in their suffering." (Exodus 2:11) His first intentional act is to leave the palace, walk among his brothers and sisters, and witness their pain. "And he saw an Egyptian beating one of his Hebrew brothers." (Exodus 2:11) In defense of his brother, he rises and kills the Egyptian. While the tradition debates whether his actions were justified, what cannot be ignored is that from his perch of royal power, he chooses to see, and like Abraham he can neither ignore nor rationalize away what is in front of him. He witnesses injustice and acts to repair it, even when to do so is likely to hold dire consequences for him personally.

Ultimately, Moses's relentless nonindifference leads him into confrontations not only with Egyptian taskmasters, Midianite shepherds, Pharaoh, and the Israelites themselves—but, like Abraham, with God as well. When God, in the midst of bestowing the Torah to Moses as the Jewish people's emissary atop Mount Sinai, notices that they have despaired of Moses's return and built a Golden Calf as an idol to worship, the response is swift and severe. God cuts off the unique revelatory moment with the words, "Go down," and informs Moses of a new divine plan to wipe out the Children of Israel and begin a new people with Moses as the founding patriarch.

Moses does not consider the suggestion for a moment. He immediately begins to argue with God and pleads for a reversal, offering the ultimatum: Forgive their sins, "and if not, erase me, please, from the book You have written." (Exodus 32:32) God has promised to exempt Moses from the suffering and sin that surrounds him, to make him royalty as he was in his youth—this time in a palace built in partnership with God. Moses's response is unequivocal: If you want me, then you have to know that I am not the type of person to remain indifferent to the suffering of my people.

Generations later, the rabbis of the Talmud drew this scene in even sharper relief, amplifying the fearlessness with which Moses confronts God: "Moses took hold of the Holy One, blessed be He, like a man who seizes his fellow by his garment and said before Him: Sovereign of the Universe, I will not let You go until You forgive and pardon them." (BT Berakhot 32a)

The same sense of obligation that motivates Moses to see and respond to the plight of Jews under their Egyptian slave masters is what subsequently leads him to defend them against God's wrath. No matter what is offered him, whom (or Whom) he must confront, or the risk of such confrontation to him personally, Moses is defined by the inability to avert his eyes from the plight of those people, however flawed, with whom he shares a collective bond.

It is this quality that the tradition uses to explain one of Moses's signature acts: smashing the first set of tablets he receives from God after witnessing the sin of the people in building the Golden Calf. The rabbis wonder how he could have acted so boldly (seemingly sacrilegiously) on his own authority. These were the Tablets of God, after all, and nowhere was he given direction or permission to break them. Where could he possibly have found the hutzpah? Their answer is that Moses smashes the tablets immediately after arguing with God to spare the lives of his people and to continue to uphold the covenant with the Jewish nation.

A straightforward reading of the biblical text would see this as a sharp shift in mood. After defending the people to God, Moses now turns to them with the righteous fury of a spiritual leader who recognizes the necessity of holding them accountable for their sins. The Talmudic rabbis, however, offer a different reading of this sequence of events. For them, Moses smashes the tablets not in a fit of indignation and judgment but as a continuation of the same protective impulse that led him to defend them against God's wrath. "When Moses saw the sin of the Jewish people he said, 'How shall I give these tablets to Israel? I shall be obligating them to major commandments, and make them liable to the penalty of death! . . . Rather, I shall take hold of them and break them.'" (Avot de-Rabbi Natan, Chapter 2)

Rather than viewing himself exclusively as a conduit of divine law or as a tool of divine justice—which would be understandable given his forty-day mountaintop sojourn with God—Moses's first thought is for the well-being of the people, irrespective of their sinful behavior. Better to destroy the Torah, he reasons, and give them time to prepare themselves to receive it again, than bestow it when they are not ready and it will make them liable to the death penalty. According to this interpretation, Moses understands that one value brooks no compromise: to be his brothers' and sisters' keeper. It does not matter who is ultimately responsible for the threat to his people. In the case of the Golden Calf, they clearly have brought it upon themselves. The agent of danger is also immaterial, whether it is Pharaoh, or God, or, as in this case, the Torah itself.

Moses's uncompromising vision and refusal to remain indifferent establish the template for the later prophetic tradition. Whether attempting to combat the abuse of power by the monarchy, as in the case of Nathan and David or Elijah and Ahab, or calling upon an all-too-forgetful people to take up the cause of their needy brethren, as in the case of Isaiah, Jeremiah, Amos, and Micah, the prophets, like Moses, are role models for walking in Abraham's path.

THE LOST PROPHET

Jonah is the countermodel to the prophetic tradition: a book about a prophet who has lost his way, and who, because of his "jealousy" for God, refuses to take responsibility for the needs of others. Forcing him to see, and obligating him to overcome this indifference, is the central message of his biblical story.

God sees the sins of the city of Nineveh and the consequent punishment that perpetuating this behavior will provoke and charges his prophet with a mission to warn and save them. "Go at once to Nineveh, that great city, and proclaim judgment upon it; for their wickedness has come before me." (Jonah 1:1) Jonah wants the people punished for their sins against God, is reluctant to carry God's message, and attempts to run away, literally and figuratively—"Jonah, however, started out to flee to Tarshish from the Lord's service" (1:3)—until divine machinations and admonitions finally force him to be present and take responsibility for saving Nineveh. While Jonah's mission is a great success, and the people of Nineveh repent and are saved, Jonah is deeply distressed. "This displeased Jonah greatly, and he was grieved. He prayed to the Lord, saying, 'Oh Lord! Isn't this just what I said when I was still in my own country? That is why I fled beforehand to Tarshish. For I know that You are a compassionate and gracious God, slow to anger, abounding in kindness, renouncing punishment. Please, Lord, take my life, for I would rather die than live." (4:1–3)

Jonah believes that his loyalty to God requires of him to save God from Godself, to help God overcome the divine flaws of compassion and graciousness. The lesson of the book is that it is not God who is in need of transformation, but Jonah. "Should not I have pity on Nineveh, that great city, where there are more than a hundred and twenty thousand persons that cannot discern between their right hand and their left hand, and also much cattle?" (Jonah 4:10–11)

In an interesting twist, God here echoes the voice of Abraham pleading for the lives of the people of Sodom, reminding Jonah of this core Jewish value. Cynical and embittered, Jonah has given up on his moral obligation toward his fellow human beings, and here it is God who must bring him back to the "way of the Lord."

A SEEING GOD

Seeing, listening, and responding become the dominant motifs in the character of God as portrayed throughout the Bible. The God of Abraham exhibits the ethic of responsibility on a national scale in response to the suffering of the Jewish people enslaved in Egypt. Calling out to Moses in the encounter at the burning bush, God's motivation for liberating the Jews is described in precisely this language: "And the Lord said: 'I have certainly seen the affliction of My people in Egypt, and have heard their cry because of their taskmasters; yes, I know their sufferings; and I am coming down to deliver them out of the hand of the Egyptians and to bring them out of that land to a good and spacious land, a land flowing with milk and honey. . . . And now, behold, the cry of the children of Israel has come before Me; moreover I have seen the oppression wherewith the Egyptians oppress them. Come, therefore, I will send you to Pharaoh, and you shall free My people, the children of Israel, from Egypt." (Exodus 3:7–10)

With the revelation at Sinai, the biblical God begins to embody nonindifference in the form of divine legislation: enlisting the Jewish people to form a community of seeing and nonindifference. In the laws concerning the treatment of society's most vulnerable, the biblical language characterizes God as their keeper, the paradigm of one who sees, hears, cares, and responds.

> And a stranger you shall neither wrong nor oppress; for you were strangers in the land of Egypt. You shall not afflict any widow or orphan. If you afflict them in any way—for if they cry at all unto Me, I will surely hear their cry—My wrath shall wax hot, and I will kill you with the sword; and your wives shall be widows, and your children fatherless. . . . If you take your neighbor's garment as a pledge, you shall restore it unto him before the sun goes down; for that is his only clothing, the sole covering for his skin; in what else shall he sleep? And it shall come to pass, when he cries unto Me, that I will hear; for I am gracious (*hanun*). (Exodus 22:20–23; 25–26)

The God of nonindifference shapes Jewish law even more directly through the commandment of *imitatio dei*—the obligation to walk in God's ways by mirroring God's values and practices. The Hebrew word translated as "gracious" (*hanun*)—associated here with seeing, hearing, and empathic knowledge—is central to the Talmudic understanding of God's personality. This understanding draws upon the moment in the book of Exodus when Moses asks to "know" God "by name." (Exodus 33:17) In response, he is met with a kind of incantation, the content of which is a litany of divine attributes: "Adonai, Adonai, gracious (*hanun*) and compassionate God, slow to anger and filled with kindness and truth." (Exodus 34:6–7) This formula was understood by the Talmudic rabbis as an invocation of God's most salient and essential qualities, the qualities humanity is meant to emulate.

> What is meant by what is written: "After the Lord your God you shall follow"? Is it possible for a person to walk after

God? Behold! It has already been said, "For the Lord your God is a consuming fire." Rather, one should follow after the Holy One's characteristics: Just as God clothed the naked, as it is written, "And Lord, God, made garments of skins for the man and his wife and clothed them," so shall you clothe the naked. Just as God visited the sick, as it is written, "And the Lord appeared to him at the terebinths of Mamre," so shall you visit the sick. Just as God comforted mourners, as it is written, "And it was after the death of Abraham, God blessed Yitzhak, his son," so shall you comfort mourners. Just as God buried corpses, as it is written, "And God buried him in the valley," so shall you bury corpses. (BT Sotah 14a)

The rabbis grappled with the question of how finite human beings, confined to the realm of the physical, can be said in any meaningful way to *follow* an infinite, transcendent being. How is this mitzvah to be fulfilled? Their resolution is to focus the conception and practice of *imitatio dei*: "Be like God: just as God is gracious [*hanun*] and compassionate, so too you shall be gracious [*hanun*] and compassionate." (BT Shabbat 133b)

"DO NOT REMAIN INDIFFERENT": THE LAWS OF LOST PROPERTY

To walk in God's ways, to see oneself as one's brothers' and sisters' keeper, is also translated into a legal principle governing the interaction between individuals in the public sphere. "You shall not see your fellow's ox or sheep gone astray, and remain indifferent. You must take it back to your fellow . . . and so shall you do with his ass, and so shall you do with his garment: you must not remain indifferent." (Deuteronomy 22:1–3)

The biblical context of lost property initially seems to be a relatively insignificant place to locate so central a tenet. Upon closer examination, however, it becomes clear that the laws of lost property play a central role in ensuring that the public space is safe for all who traverse through it. Within Jewish tradition, criminal and tort law are the first lines of defense against unbridled self-interest. However, preventing harm and providing legal recourse are not sufficient. The public arena becomes safe only when it is a space of "fellow keepers," in which individuals recognize their responsibility not merely to refrain from harming others but to care for and to respond to their needs. This is the aim of the laws of lost property.

In the course of daily life, individuals inevitably become separated at times from their possessions. In the private domain, one's property is protected by doors and fences, and the chain of continuous possession and subsequent ownership is more easily maintained. One who does not respect this chain is clearly identified as a thief. However, this is not the case in the public domain, a space devoid of personal demarcations. We need to enter the public space regularly: How do we ensure that this act is neither a cause for anxiety nor a framework for repeated loss?

In the Torah, the laws of lost property shape a consensus of both behavior and consciousness in which fellow citizens do not enter the public domain seeking either to ignore or to benefit from the misfortunes of others. What could be more natural than simply looking the other way when coming into contact with a lost piece of property? Who needs the hassle of trying to run down the owner? It is all too easy to say that, as a busy person, I do not have time to be my brother's keeper. Alternatively, I could view such a moment as a prospect for personal gain. Who knows, I might reason, perhaps it is meant to belong to me? Perhaps it is a gift from God! In both cases, the lens is actually a mirror: when I look at someone else's loss, I can see only myself, my needs, and interests.

For this reason, Jewish tradition commands: "You shall not see your fellow's ox or sheep gone astray, and remain indifferent. You must take it back to your fellow." Commanded to walk in the way of the Lord by doing what is just and right, we are therefore compelled to see our fellows' needs and respond.

A parallel to this legislation is found in the book of Exodus, which expands the scope of a person's obligation to see, care, and respond to one's fellow to include one's enemy. "If you come upon your enemy's ass or ox running astray, you must surely bring it back to him." (Exodus 23:4) The Jewish Bible does not call for the love of one's enemy along the lines of the Gospel of Matthew, but it does demand the extension of one's moral responsibility to be others' keepers. When it comes to following in "the way of the Lord," the distinction between friend and foe becomes irrelevant. The ethic of nonindifference, of doing what is "just and right," sometimes requires smashing the mirror of self-interest.

"DO NOT STAND IDLY BY": JEWISH BYSTANDER LAWS

This standard of nonindifference, while mentioned explicitly in the context of the laws of lost property, is the underlying principle behind much of Jewish ethics. Another application is found in the commandment to "not stand idly by the blood of your neighbor" (Leviticus 19:16), which the rabbinic tradition interpreted to mean active assistance when one sees another person in danger. "Our rabbis taught: whence do we know that if a man sees his fellow drowning, mauled by beasts, or attacked by robbers, that he is bound to save him? From the verse: 'You shall not stand idly by the blood of your neighbor.'" (BT Sanhedrin 73a)

Any danger or injustice threatening one's neighbor, whether within the public or private domain, is one's business. If it is within one's power to eliminate this danger or injustice, one is obligated to do so. We are all our neighbors' keepers.

In an interesting, albeit potentially problematic, extension of the principle of nonindifference, Jewish law also obligates intervention when one sees someone harming him- or herself through sin. "If one observes that a person committed a sin or walks in a way that is not good, it is a duty to bring the erring person back to the right path and point out that he is wronging himself by his evil courses, as it is said, 'You shall surely rebuke your neighbor.' (Leviticus 19:17) He who rebukes another, whether for offenses against the rebuker himself or for sins against God, should administer the rebuke in private, speak to the offender gently and tenderly, and point out that he is only speaking for the wrongdoer's own good. . . . Whoever is in a position to prevent wrongdoing and does not do so, is responsible for the iniquity of all the wrongdoing he might have prevented." (Maimonides, *Mishneh Torah*, Hilkhot Yesodei HaTorah 6:7)

The principle common to all these cases is the obligation of nonindifference. One does not walk through the world in pursuit of self-interest or self-preservation alone, but in pursuit of extending and maximizing justice and good.

JUSTICE, DIGNITY, AND THE LAWS OF *TZEDAKAH*

Perhaps the Jewish tradition's most significant extension of the nonindifference principle is embodied in myriad laws associated with *tzedakah*, often translated as "charity," but which in its original literal sense actually means "justice." In fact, the commandment (mitzvah) of *tzedakah* is connected by the rabbis to the core of what it means to do the just and right thing, and thus to walk in the ways of God. (BT Yevamot 79a) In his codification of Jewish law, Maimonides describes its central significance for Jewish identity: "We are obligated to be more scrupulous in fulfilling the commandment of tzedakah than any other positive commandment, because tzedakah is the sign of the righteous person, the seed of Abraham our Father, as it is said, 'For I know him, that he will command his children . . . to do righteousness.'" (Maimonides, *Mishneh Torah*, Hilkhot Matnot Aniyim 10:1)

The laws of *tzedakah* obligate individuals to transcend self-interest and adopt a view of themselves, and by extension of their property, as being in service of others who are in need—in a sense, to the extent of even belonging to them. "If there be among you a needy person, one of your brothers, within any of your gates, in your land which the Lord your God gives you, you shall not harden your heart, nor shut your hand from your needy brother; but thou shall surely open your hand unto him, and shall surely lend him sufficient for his need in that which he lacks. . . . For there will never cease to be needy ones in your land, which is why I command you: open your hand to the poor and needy kinsman in your land." (Deuteronomy 15:7–11)

Responsibility for the needy results from the simple fact that they exist. While the Bible itself posits that poverty may be a consequence of sin, it also emphasizes that this in no way excuses others from the responsibility to help the impoverished. (Deuteronomy 15:4–6) The simple reality that we are each other's keepers generates a standing obligation. From this starting point, the biblical laws of *tzedakah* mandate a comprehensive and intricate system of tithing; making part of one's field accessible to the poor so that they can freely gather a portion of the produce; interest-free loans; and ultimately, by the Talmudic period, direct almsgiving.

Within this elaborate system, a strong recurring motif is that one's responsibility for *tzedakah* extends beyond the alleviation of physical hunger. What is required is a more complex obligation to see the destitute person in his or her totality. Nonindifference demands a nuanced sense of the problems the needy face and the construction of a system of assistance commensurate with these needs. Of particular importance in *tzedakah* law is that the destitute maintain their dignity throughout the process of receiving aid. As a result, in the Bible, produce was not passed from the owner to the poor, but was left in the field for them to take. "And when you reap the harvest of your land, you shall not reap the entire corner of your field, nor shall you gather the gleaning of your harvest. And you shall not glean your vineyard, nor gather the fallen fruit of your vineyard; you shall leave them for the poor and for the stranger: I am the Lord your God." (Leviticus 19:9–10)

This gave birth, in later Jewish law, to the value of giving alms in secret, with the highest form being anonymous giving, in which neither contributor nor recipient knows the other's identity. "One who gives charity to the poor without knowing to whom he gave and without the poor person knowing from whom he received. For this is an observance of the mitzvah for its sake alone. This [type of giving was] exemplified by the secret chamber that existed in the Temple. The righteous would make donations there in secret and poor people of distinguished lineage would derive their livelihood from it in secret." (Maimonides, Hilkhot Matnot Aniyim, *Mishnah Torah* 10:8)

Moreover, when giving does occur face to face, the giver is obligated not only to act generously but also to project a generous spirit. Here the obligation of nonindifference to the totality of a person's needs is brought into pointed and vivid relief. "Whenever a person gives charity to a poor person with an unpleasant countenance and with his face buried in the earth, he loses and destroys his merit even if he gives him 1,000 gold pieces. Instead, he should greet him with a pleasant countenance and with happiness, commiserating with him about his troubles, as [Job 30:25] states: 'Did I not weep for those who face difficult times; did not my soul feel sorrow for the destitute?' And he should speak to him words of sympathy and comfort, as [Job 29:13] states: 'I would bring joy to a widow's heart.'" (Maimonides, Hilkhot Matnot Aniyim, *Mishnah Torah* 10:4)

A second prominent concern in the rabbinic development of *tzedakah* law was ensuring that the required assistance was "sufficient for his need"—not standardized but rather left as subjective, varying from case to case. To see the other and care for him or her requires a customized response to each individual's particular circumstances. "Our Rabbis taught: 'Sufficient for his need' [implies] you are commanded to maintain him, but you are not commanded to make him rich; 'in that which he lacks' [includes] even a horse to ride upon and a slave to run before him. It was related about Hillel the Elder that he bought for a certain poor man who was of a good family a horse to ride upon and a servant to run before him. On one occasion he could not find a slave to run before him, so he himself ran before him for three miles. Our Rabbis taught: It once happened that the people of Upper Galilee bought for a poor member of a good family of Sepphoris a pound of meat every day. . . . The place was a small village and every day a beast had to be spoiled for his sake. (BT Ketubot 67b)

To be another's keeper in the eyes of the rabbis meant to shift one's gaze away from theoretical or fixed notions of justice toward the recognition that each case has its own just result. This is the sensitivity and acuity of nonindifference.

THE SABBATICAL YEAR: MODELING NONINDIFFERENCE

The imperative of nonindifference gives rise to a concern not only with the response of the individual at the moment that we see another's need, but also with facilitating a social reality that maximizes the possibility of individuals to become seeing people. How does one create an overall societal predisposition toward nonindifference?

The biblical narrative, with its archetypal heroes and preponderance of laws, is clearly concerned with addressing this question. The Bible, in a sense, went one stage farther by instituting a number of experimental social frameworks designed to facilitate seeing by removing some of the boundaries that can lead to alienation and, consequently, indifference. Primary among these is the institution of the Sabbatical Year, with rituals and laws that emphasize different aspects of releasing personal ownership. (The Hebrew word *shmitah*, another name for the Sabbatical Year, means "release.")

> "When you enter the land that I assign you, the land shall observe a sabbath of the Lord. Six years you may sow your field, and six years you may prune your vineyard, and gather in the yield. But in the seventh year the land shall have a sabbath of complete rest, a sabbath of the Lord; you shall not sow your field, or prune your vineyard. You shall not reap the after-growth of your harvest or father the grapes of your untrimmed vines; it shall be a year of complete rest for the land. But you may eat whatever the land during its sabbath will produce—you, your male and female slaves, the hired and bound laborers who live with you, and your cattle and the beasts in your land may eat all its yield. (Leviticus 25:2–7)

The sabbatical described in Leviticus constructs a reality in which the walls of ownership are broken down and all members of the community enter into the fields together as equals. Normally, the poor are allowed only restricted access—to the corners and what falls or is left behind—but every seven years, the hierarchy of ownership is dissolved, social status leveled. Less fortunate fellow citizens, who are considered "silent partners" in all Jewish fields within the normative laws of *tzedakah*, now become full partners in a shared land.

As distinct from the sabbatical laws in Leviticus, the sabbatical laws of Exodus present a different paradigm in which the poor are given total access to all Jewish fields. But in this version, rather than collecting side by side with the poor, owners are prohibited from collecting any of the produce of their own land. What emerges from the sabbatical of Exodus is a sharply constructed exercise in role reversal. "Six years you shall sow your land, and gather in its yield; but the seventh year you shall let it rest and lie fallow. Let the needy among your people eat of it, and what they leave let the beast eat." (Exodus 23:10–11)

One's ability (or willingness) to see others is highly conditioned by the range of one's experience. The landowner is usually on the inside, while the poor are on the outside, waiting and hoping for whatever access they can obtain. The landowner never sees their side, does not know the experience of not having access to a field. The extent of social contact and camaraderie is limited, bound by the economic barriers that divide people. The sabbaticals of Leviticus and Exodus present two models of repair. One way is to create a sacred time free of conventional social hierarchy (everyone stands together in the field); another is role reversal. Both are designed to enhance individuals' overall sensitivity to the position of vulnerable others with whom they share the public domain. Identifying with those on the outside looking in is likely to have a transformative effect on the insiders' attitudes toward those on the outside.

In many ways, this is the core idea behind the most significant and frequent Jewish holiday, the Sabbath. Every seventh day, Jews are commanded to create a sacred time in which the distinctions between the wealthy and the poor, the powerful and the powerless, are dissolved. The powerful are obligated to rest, according to the book of Deuteronomy, solely to ensure that those over whom they have dominion are given respite from their labor. "Observe the Sabbath day and keep it holy. . . . You shall not do any work . . . so that your male and female slave may rest as you do." (Deuteronomy 5:12–14) Echoing again the principle of *imitatio dei*, the God who was not indifferent to the oppression of the Israelites in Egypt commands the reenactment of the Exodus story on a weekly basis. Just as God stood with the powerless in the Exodus, the powerful stand with the powerless every seventh day, creating a society in which the powerful and the powerless are equal, even if only for an aspirational twenty-five hours per week.

ZONING FOR NONINDIFFERENCE

As Jewish society moved away from a purely agrarian model to an increasingly urban one, and the laws of *tzedakah* took on the predominant form of almsgiving, the Talmudic rabbis struggled to ensure that within this new context indifference would not hold sway. One creative answer was through an innovative zoning policy.

At the time (second century CE), the standard urban home was built around a common courtyard, with one central gate opening into the main thoroughfare. Such homes housed several families. If any of the families sharing the courtyard made an improvement, they had the ability to tax the other members to defray the cost, as long as the improvement was accepted as a benefit shared by all. One such improvement the rabbis discussed was a gatehouse, the purpose of which was to separate the common courtyard from the public domain. The higher level of privacy and security it afforded was what recommended it as a benefit, making it, according to the *Mishneh*, a taxable item.

Why, then, does the Talmud's anonymous editorial voice raise a strong objection? "But is a gatehouse really a benefit? What about that pious man, with whom Elijah the Prophet would regularly converse? He built a gatehouse, and Elijah did not converse with him further." (BT Baba Batra 7b)

Apparently, the later Talmudic rabbis are privy to a story that asserts that gatehouses are not the pure benefit the earlier statement makes them out to be. Elijah the prophet, who often functions in rabbinic literature as an angelic liaison between the physical and metaphysical realms, communicating a divine perspective on human affairs—a voice representing, perhaps, the rabbis' attempts to imagine a divine appraisal of their own activities—appears to strongly disapprove of them. A place that Elijah refuses to be is by definition a place of which God wants no part. What is the great conflict between piety and the construction of a gatehouse?

According to the medieval commentator Rashi, Elijah severed ties with the pious gatehouse builder because gatehouses create an extra physical barrier between the courtyard and the public, and thus "cut off from view those calling out [that is, the needy, out in the street, calling for *tzedakah*], and their voices are not heard." Thus we learn that, while the values of privacy and security might seem like reasonable concerns, they cannot be permitted to impinge on our responsibility to see and respond to those in need. And to see, we must maintain an open field of vision and access for the poor. The poor may not be prevented from entering the courtyard. They cannot be made invisible, and their voices cannot be silenced, for these are circumstances that promote and reinforce indifference. They must be able to be seen and heard, so that those living in the courtyard may be made aware of their presence and thus be capable of responding to their need. For only when one's home becomes a place of nonindifference, open and responsive to the pressing reality of human need, can it become a divine dwelling.

The Talmud concludes that it is permitted to build a gatehouse, but only if it is constructed in a way that allows free and open access to the poor (for example, with handles on the outside and without locks). A house that God might want to visit is one whose inhabitants are capable of seeing and hearing the poor. A Jewish society is one in which everyone is obligated to be able to see and be seen. Sometimes, the Talmud here teaches, the physical organization of shared space encourages an insidiously passive form of hiding and ignoring. The obligation of nonindifference is not only to see but also to create a society in which seeing is possible. If the sabbatical laws invoked a model of sacred time based on the principle of nonindifference, here the rabbis define sacred space as nonindifferent space as well.

To learn from the failure of Cain, Jewish tradition requires its adherents to respond to the call "Where is your brother or sister, and what is the status of his or her needs?" with the answer,

"I am my brother's keeper, I see my sister's needs, and I am working on it." For anyone who accepts the obligation to keep the way of the Lord by doing what is just and right, this is the only appropriate answer.

CONFRONTING THE BIBLE'S MIXED ETHICAL LEGACY

Now, were this the whole story, this book could now happily be concluded. But the story of Jewish ethics is admittedly more problematic. As I will outline in great detail in the following chapters, the obligatory standard of nonindifference woven into the tradition through stories, cultural heroes, and laws is accompanied by parallel themes of significantly darker hues. The same Abraham who protests heroically the injustice at Sodom hands over his wife Sarah to an Egyptian Pharaoh to save his own life (Genesis 12:11–13), casts out his son Ishmael to die in the desert (Genesis 21:6–14), and offers his son Isaac as a sacrifice to a deity who has seemingly forgotten, along with Abraham, the imperative of the judge of all the earth to do justice. (Genesis 22)

As to the rest of the Bible, the record is no less uneven. The same Moses who is the paradigm of a "brother's keeper" descends from the mountain following the sin of the Golden Calf and summarily executes three thousand of his kin. (Exodus 32:26–29) The same God who commands nonindifference to the plight of the downtrodden permits, and even commands, the subjugation of non-Jewish slaves (Leviticus 25:44–46) and the genocidal treatment of civilian captives of war from among the seven Canaanite nations. (Deuteronomy 20:16–17) The same God who sees the Jews in Egypt and the citizens of Nineveh also wipes out the world with a flood (Genesis 7), sanctions the collective torture of Egyptian innocents (Exodus 7:19–10:29), and murders the Egyptians' first-born sons. (Exodus 12:29) God is not merely a model for mercy and kindness—"The Lord! The Lord! A God compassionate and gracious, slow to anger, abounding in kindness and faithfulness, extending kindness to the thousandth generation, forgiving iniquity, transgression, and sin"—but is also a model for vengeance who promises jealously to extract payment for sins upon generations to come—"yet He does not remit all punishment, but visits the iniquity of parents on children, and children's children, upon the third and the fourth generation." (Exodus 34:6–7)

Indeed, the laws of lost property, which gave birth to the commandment of nonindifference in the first place, are limited by many within the rabbinic tradition to the lost property of Jews, and allow Jews to be indifferent to the needs of non-Jews. "Rav Hama bar Guria said in the name of Rav, 'From whence do we know that it is permitted to keep the lost property of a non-Jew? For it says: "And so too shall you do with anything that your brother [*ahikha*] loses and you find." (Deuteronomy 22:3) To your brother you must return [a lost object], and to the non-Jew you do not return [a lost object].'" (BT Baba Kama 113b)

In truth, Judaism, like all religious traditions, can be likened to "a tale of two cities," with the best of stories and the worst of stories, the most just and the least just of laws. The core argument of this book is that this inconsistency is not an accident, the product of inadequate editing, but rather the result of an internal battle within religion about the essence of religion, with each voice undermining the other. One aspect of religious life is defined by the notion that to walk in God's ways is to act with justice and compassion. Yet, at the same time, religion has a shadow side that suggests a different way of walking with God. The challenge is to identify the cause and nature of this tension, which I term religion's autoimmune disease, and to investigate the tradition for resources with which to combat and defeat it.

Religion is currently engaged in a cultural and ideological war over its essential identity. The question that religiously committed people must face is which collection of verses to quote, emphasize, and weave into the tapestry of religion's essence. Which narrative will ultimately prevail? Which passages will nurture and comprise the beating heart of faith, and which will be relegated to the ideological dumping ground of verses that, according to the Talmudic adage, "never were nor were ever meant to be implemented, but were written only as objects of theoretical study." (BT Sanhedrin 71a)

This internal cultural war over the moral soul of Judaism is not merely being waged between competing chapters and verses. Precisely because it defines the essence of ethical responsibility in terms of seeing the other and responding as needed, Judaism exposes itself to being undermined by the darker dimensions of religious consciousness, which attack the ability to see and as a result foster indifference and moral blindness. This inner weakness provides a fertile soil for Judaism's autoimmune diseases to take root, as I will show in the next chapter.

———

CHAPTER TWO

GOD INTOXICATION
AND GOD MANIPULATION

The devil can cite Scripture for his purpose.
—William Shakespeare, *The Merchant of Venice*

AS MORE AND MORE people are being killed daily in the name of one god or another, I often wonder about the religious sensibilities of these pious perpetrators of murder and pain. What moves people to believe that God loves and rewards such vicious acts? Where is the piety in blowing up another's house of worship? What moves the religious leader to order or sanction all wars that serve his or her religious or political community? What moves the individual who in the name of God is so quick to judge others as an abomination? What gives so many people of faith the license to intolerance?

Like most people, I have, at different moments in my life, encountered people who in the name of their God felt empowered to hurt others. One of my earliest experiences with such a person was when, as an eighteen-year-old student during my first year boarding in an Orthodox yeshiva, I was the only one not to be invited to the office of the dean of students. During the first few weeks of studies, the dean met with every one of the sixty-five first-year students to get to know them and to inquire how both he and the school could make the transition as positive as possible. I was accepted to the school because I did well on the entrance exam, but my last name tainted me in the eyes of the dean. My father was an Orthodox rabbi who held views that many in the community felt to be unacceptable, and even heretical. When asked by my fellow students why he snubbed me in this way, the dean replied, "He is a Hartman, and I have nothing to say to him."

At the time, when told his response, I came back with age-appropriate bravado: "He is right! We have nothing to say to each other, and I do not want to meet him either." And so began an ongoing process, over four years, of shunning and alienation on the part of the seminary's leadership.

While there is nothing like a good shunning to make you a better person, more tolerant, and less quick to judge those who are different, it was only years later that I began to reflect on what might cause such behavior. Here was a man widely viewed as pious and holy and a model of religious emulation, whose religious ideology prompted him to embarrass and humiliate a young student under his care. Known to be devout and kind, he seemed to be acting in ways that were antithetical to who he was. It was as if I activated within him a darker side. Or, more accurately, I activated within his religious sensibilities a darker side, which both allowed him and propelled him to injustice.

MORALITY AND FAITH: WHERE DOES RELIGION GO WRONG?

Given the prominence of ethical aspirations and obligations within monotheistic faiths, how do we understand the common disconnect between moral excellence and the life of faith? While moral failure is certainly not the exclusive province of the religious, this fact does little to recommend either religious traditions in general or God in particular as potent forces of progress for humanity. The fact that believers are no worse than the general human population may bring comfort to some. But it can hardly be said to bring comfort to the leaders of religious traditions, who see their *raison d'etre* as being catalysts for the highest levels of human aspiration and achievement, or even to a biblical God whose express purpose in selecting Abraham was "that he may instruct his posterity to keep the way of the Lord by doing what is just and right." (Genesis 18:19)

While there are multiple causes for the moral inadequacy that so often typifies human existence, a significant and largely unobserved challenge lies squarely within religion itself. We must acknowledge that many religious systems, while commanding their adherents to act morally, also cultivate perspectives and predispositions that undermine this very goal. This inner conflict between faith in God and the moral imperative to become people who are not indifferent is at the core of religion's autoimmune disease.

This is not to deny that many believers certainly use the tradition in distorted and distorting ways, focusing on some parts of it to the exclusion of others. This is the type of piety that so frustrated the prophets: scrupulous performance of the rituals (fasting, sacrifices), while ignoring the commandments governing their obligations toward other humans. However, as we saw in the previous chapter, the devil is not always so easily detectable, and often comes armed with chapter and verse. The tradition provides him with all the ammunition he needs, and indeed he rarely need look any further.

To understand the impact of God on the sphere of human morality, then, requires both a diagnosis of the nature of the autoimmune disease to which religious individuals are so often susceptible and an exploration of the places in which the tradition itself presents symptoms of the same condition.

Monotheistic religions' autoimmune disease takes two primary forms, God Intoxication (or God-induced indifference) and God Manipulation (or God-sanctioned indifference). For the God-Intoxicated person, the awareness of living in the presence of the one transcendent God demands an all-consuming attention that can exhaust one's ability to see the needs of other human beings. This religious personality is defined by strict non-indifference to God. The more we walk with God, the less room we have to be aware of the human condition in general, and consequently, our moral sensibilities become attenuated.

A second manifestation of religion's autoimmune disease, God Manipulation, aligns the identity and will of the One with the interests and agendas of those who lay claim to God's special love. Antithetical to God Intoxication, in which God's transcendence shifts our vision away from humanity toward the transcendent One, here the passionate yearning to be loved by the transcendent One unleashes a sinful impulse to control the transcendent. In a paradoxical manner, monotheism, which sought to uproot idolatry, gives birth to perhaps the greatest idolatry of all, the idolatry of human self-intoxication, an idolatry in which God is drafted in the service of human self-interest. Within this way of thinking, we may embrace the obligation to love our neighbors as ourselves, while redefining neighbors to include not those among whom we live but rather the much smaller circle of those who share our particular set of religious beliefs. God Manipulation extends a blanket exemption from truly seeing anyone outside our religious community.

THE BINDING OF ISAAC AND THE INTOXICATION OF ABRAHAM

The Judaic paradigm of God-induced indifference is the iconic binding of Isaac (*akeidah*). "And after these things God tested Abraham, and said, 'Abraham.' And he responded, 'Here I am.' And He said, 'Take, please, your son, your only son, whom you love, Isaac. And go to the land of Moriah, and offer him there as a burnt offering on one of the mountains I will show you.' And Abraham rose in the morning, and saddled his ass, and took two of his young men with him, and Isaac his son." (Genesis 22:1–3)

God's command to Abraham to kill his son, and Abraham's response—*hineni*, "Here I am"—had a profound impact not only on Isaac but also on monotheistic faith in general, as Jon Levenson has observed in his book *The Death and Resurrection of the Beloved Son*. What is so striking about this moment is the lack of hesitation: the moment Abraham hears the voice of God, it is as if his capacity for critical thought shuts down. He does not consider his moral responsibility toward his son, nor does he debate whether to adhere to the divine commandment not to commit murder. The conversation never reaches that point, because there is no conversation. God Intoxication has already compromised his faculties. The moment he hears God's commanding voice, he ceases to see the boy standing next to him. Abraham's personality—his desires, values, and commitments—disappears the moment the word of God penetrates his consciousness. His intoxication with the divine eclipses all human concerns.

God commands the ethical, obligating us to see and not remain indifferent. Yet God's very presence can exert such a powerful gravitational force as to completely shift the rules of the game, the parameters of what we are able, or allow ourselves, to see. "I set God before me at all times." (Psalm 16:8) This is the essential feature of the autoimmune disease of God Intoxication.

Much ink has been spilled over the centuries in an attempt to comprehend the cause, and the nature, of Abraham's unhesitating *hineni*. While the text of the *akeidah* is obviously open to interpretation, crucial to our present discussion is its dominant legacy as a model of religious piety worthy of emulation, which can be traced throughout the ages. The tradition of God

Intoxication lives on far beyond the story of the *akeidah* itself to become a prominent and permanent feature of religious life. In the Jewish tradition, Abraham's moment of all-encompassing nonindifference to God serves as the foundation for demanding divine nonindifference to the needs of the Jewish people. In a kind of reverse *imitatio dei*, at the pinnacle of the High Holiday liturgy of Rosh Hashanah, we plead with the divine to mirror the behavior of Abraham:

> Remember, on our behalf, Lord our God, the covenant, the kindness, and the oath that you swore to Abraham our Father on Mount Moriah. Please see [remember] the binding (akeidah) that Abraham bound his son on the altar, and over-rided his compassion [toward Isaac] in order to do your will with a whole heart. Likewise, let your compassion override your anger toward us, and in your great goodness remove your anger from your people, and from your city, and from your inheritance." (Traditional Rosh Hashanah prayer book)

"WITH ALL YOUR SOUL": AKIVA'S *AKEIDAH*

This model of God Intoxication finds its most powerful exemplar in the Talmudic figure of Rabbi Akiva. Interpreting the second biblical verse of Judaism's most central prayer and declaration of faith, the Shema—"Hear, Israel, the Lord is our God, the Lord is One. And you shall love the Lord your God with all your heart, and with all your soul, and with all your might," (Deuteronomy 6:4–5)—Rabbi Akiva argues that "with all your soul" obligates us to be willing, under certain circumstances, to sacrifice our very lives on the altar of love of God. Rabbi Akiva himself ultimately puts this teaching into practice in his own life, when he is tortured to death by the Romans for the Hadrianic crime of teaching Torah. As the moment of his death approached, the time for reciting the Shema arrived. His students were puzzled by the steadfastness of his faith, declaring his love for God even as God had seemingly abandoned him:

> His disciples said to him: "Our teacher, even to this point?" He said to them, "All my days I have been troubled by the verse, '. . . with all your soul,' which I have interpreted, 'even if God takes your soul.' I said to myself, 'When will I have the opportunity to fulfill this?' Now that I do have this opportunity, shall I not fulfill it?" He prolonged the reciting of the word, "one" [in "Hear, Israel, the Lord is our God, the Lord is one"], until he died. A voice came forth from heaven and declared, "How fortunate are you, Akiva, for your soul departed on 'one.'" (BT Berakhot 61b)

Rabbi Akiva was in search of his own *akeidah* moment in which he could joyfully declare *hineni*: "I am here. With total faith, I willingly transcend all human concern and offer my life to You." God Intoxication creates individuals who yearn to show indifference to themselves as evidence of their nonindifference to God.

"STRIP IT OFF IN THE STREET!": SACRIFICING OTHERS

The nonindifference of the God-intoxicated, however, is characterized by a sacrificial impulse that is rarely directed exclusively toward oneself. In the rabbinic tradition, we find evidence of an obligation to sacrifice others on this same altar of nonindifference to God. One such troubling instance is in a discussion of the laws of *kilayim*, a prohibition against wearing clothing made of a blend of wool and linen. This prohibition, while one of the 613 commandments, does not make it to the top of anyone's list of critical mitzvot.

The Talmud asks: What if, by mistake, one purchases a garment in which these fabrics are interwoven and discovers it only while wearing it in the middle of the street? The obvious answer would seem to be, Go home and change! It is not difficult to imagine the Talmudic debate that might unfold in response to such a ruling. Must one return home immediately, or is there some latitude? Does it depend on how far away from home one is when the discovery is made? Whether or not it is a market day would be a consideration—if returning home immediately would negatively affect the ability to provide for one's family. This type of discussion would assume and affirm the importance of *kilayim* as a mitzvah, while also placing it in the proper perspective in relation to a larger sphere of concerns with respect to human well-being.

But these rabbis choose a different tack. "Rav Yehuda said in the name of Rav: 'If one finds kilayim (a mixture of wool and linen) in one's [or, according to some manuscripts, "another's"] garment, one is to strip it off in the street.'" (BT Berakhot 19b) A person who discovers she or he or another person is wearing *kilayim* must remove the offending garment without hesitation. Walk naked in the street, these rabbis command, rather than walk for one moment with *kilayim*, for to ignore God's commandment is to desecrate God's name, and avoiding such desecration takes precedence over any consideration of human dignity.

This position represents a worldview, a hierarchy of values, that puts God first. "I place God before me always"—in this context, "before" can be understood in both of its main senses, as a pervasive presence in human awareness and as a priority that trumps all human needs. The two, of course, are related: the more God fills my field of vision, the more human needs recede.

The mitzvot provide multiple opportunities to give expression to—and to test—where our commitments truly lie. Is my primary loyalty to God or to human dignity? The God who resides in our midst requires us to recalibrate our moral sensibilities in response to God's consuming presence. This *kilayim*

ruling presents a model of faithfulness to God whose intent
and effect are to blind us from the shame, self-interest, social
conventions, and ethical instincts that might interfere with our
unhesitating submission to God's demands. The image of God
underlying this verdict is the God of the *akeidah*, and it both
assumes and asserts Abraham's *hineni* as the paradigm of what
it means to walk in God's path.

The conclusion of this Talmudic discussion further extends
this principle. "Said Rav Pappa to Abaye: 'How is it that for the
former generations miracles were performed, and for us miracles are not performed?'" (BT Berakhot 20a) The subtext of this
question seems to be, why is God ignoring us, not seeing and
responding to our needs? Rav Pappa wants to know the reason
why the divine presence is so much less prevalent in his life than
it was in theirs. He considers, and immediately rejects, what
must have seemed to be the most obvious possibility, at least to
a rabbinic Torah scholar. "It cannot be because of their supe-
riority in study. We study more, have more to study, are more
proficient." Rav Pappa seems to suggest, "We really deserve it!"
But even so, he laments, "When Rav Judah used to take off one
shoe [at the beginning of a fast in times of drought], rain would
fall; whereas we afflict ourselves and wail, and no notice is taken
of us." Abaye answers that the deficiency that accounts for the
present generation's distance from God stems from the fact that
"the former generations were willing to sacrifice their lives for
the sanctification of God's name; we are not."

To illustrate the greater spiritual fortitude of even fairly
recent ancestors, the Talmud proceeds to offer an example.
"There was a case of Rabbi Ada son of Akba, who saw a heathen
woman wearing a red head-dress in the street, and thinking that
she was an Israelite woman, he rose and tore it from her [because
her clothing was considered immodest]." (BT Berakhot 20a)

According to this source, God's closeness to prior generations
stemmed from their willingness to sacrifice the dignity of others

on the altar of the sanctification of God's name. They lived by the creed that if a conflict arises between God's honor and any human value, the former takes precedence. Within this religious framework, the willingness to strip off a woman's headdress in the street becomes a sign of profound religious piety.

What about her feelings? What about the humiliation she will suffer at the hands of this so-called piety? Blinded by God, we fail to see her; indeed, we are commanded not to see her. Here the moral consequences of God Intoxication come sharply into relief. It shuts down our moral instincts to such an extent that we no longer see the woman standing before us at all, just the headdress deemed offensive to God. The field of moral vision becomes reduced to one test: to exhibit my complete devotion to God by suppressing every other competing consideration.

"HAVE YOU EMERGED TO DESTROY MY WORLD?": THE INTOXICATING RELIGION OF THE CAVE

This model of God Intoxication defines the piety of another great hero of the Talmudic period, Rabbi Shimon bar Yokhai (Rashbi), who according to the Talmud was forced to flee a Roman decree of death for the crime of critiquing their famous public works. "All they have made, they made for themselves; they built marketplaces to set harlots in them; baths to rejuvenate themselves; bridges to levy tolls for them." (BT Shabbat 33b) Hearing of this public criticism, the Romans declare him liable to execution. He runs away and hides, brings his son along, and ultimately ends up in a cave. "A miracle occurred, and a carob tree and a water well were created for them. They would strip their garments and sit up to their necks in sand. . . . Thus they dwelt twelve years in the cave." (BT Shabbat 33b)

Rashbi and his son live twelve years as disembodied brains, only dressing in moments of prayer, otherwise living in a state of all-consuming intellectual contemplation. Eventually the prophet Elijah stops by to inform them that the previous emperor has died, and his decree is annulled. They emerge from what the Talmud seems to characterize as a paradise. While driven there by persecution, they find an idyllic setting apparently constructed and nurtured by God. Upon leaving their cave, they witness a man plowing and sowing his field, and cry out in contempt, "'They forsake life eternal and engage in life temporal!' Whatever they cast their eyes upon was immediately burnt up." (BT Shabbat 33b)

Encountering people who subsist not on miracles but on the toil of their labor, Rashbi and his son can see only the debasement of a life in which God does not consume the entire human field of vision. These archetypes of God Intoxication lack any capacity to tolerate, much less empathize with or care for, others living in a less God-centered universe. Guided by this mindset, they set off on a path to destroy the actual universe God created.

Is this what God wants? From the first part of the story it would seem that God is squarely on the side of Rashbi, his son, and the cave. (It was God, after all, who made the carob tree grow and the stream appear.) But instead of affirmation, God responds to them with rage. "Thereupon a Heavenly Voice cried out: 'Have you emerged to destroy My world? Return to your cave!'" (BT Shabbat 33b) With this pronouncement, God clarifies that God's primary commitment is not to the cave and all it symbolizes, but to the world. For the God of creation, who sees the world and proclaims it "very good," the dichotomy between the divine and the human is religiously false. Intoxication with God must by definition encompass God's creatures. After supporting them with miracles to allow for a life of uninterrupted Torah study, God proclaims that they have learned the wrong lessons, exiles them from God's world, and promptly sends them back into their cave.

"They returned and dwelt there twelve months, as it is written, 'The punishment of the wicked in Hell is twelve months.'"

The cave, which initially seemed to be heaven, is now described as hell, a punishment for the wicked who have become indifferent to God's world. After completing their sentence, "A Heavenly Voice then came forth and said, 'Go forth from your cave!'" They can rejoin the world, but only after the requisite period of atonement. God abhors being confined to a cave, as well as those who treat the world as antithetical to the spiritual reverie of the cave religion. God echoes the cry of the prophets: Who asked this of you? True piety is expressed not in shunning the world but by actively participating in its improvement. If it leads you to turn your back on the world—my world—it is not piety, seems to be God's message. If you insist on practicing the religion of the cave, the cave is where you will remain.

Hearing the words of God's forgiveness "they emerged from the cave. And wherever Rabbi Eliezer wounded, Rashbi healed." (BT Shabbat 33b)

It is significant to note that even God's direct intervention leads only to a partial victory. Rashbi's son, Rabbi Eliezer, is unable to hear, or perhaps to bear, this heavenly rebuke. He continues to destroy, with his gaze of fiery contempt, anyone he sees relating to God's world with what he deems to be an overly embodied, temporal orientation (that is, everyone except him and his father)—despite God's direct rejection of this religious stance. Rashbi seems to hear God's message and repent, healing the wounds his overzealous son cannot restrain himself from inflicting. However, even Rashbi's repentance is illusory, since the Talmud reports that every act of rectification for his son's havoc is accompanied by the reassurance, "My son, you and I are enough." Rashbi heals the world not because he internalizes God's message that indifference to the world constitutes indifference to God. To the contrary, he exhibits an even greater indifference: Leave them, he says, they are not even worthy of being destroyed.

This story is a testimony to the powerful attraction, and the misguided destructiveness, of God Intoxication. Who asked this of you? God demands to know, and in the tragic irony of this question lies the germ of monotheism's autoimmune disease. For in the very act of self-revelation, of making the divine presence accessible to human experience, God unleashes a spiritual virus on human beings that even God cannot control, a force that subverts God's plan for humanity while speaking in God's name. Even in the face of God's explicit command, those afflicted by God Intoxication cannot control their behavior. Paradoxically, because of the nature of this autoimmune disease, it is precisely those who pursue the most intense and consuming intimacy with God who can so often become, as a result of this very form of devotion, least able to hear God's voice.

HOW CAN YOU LEAVE OUT GOD?: A RADICAL REVISION

This zero-sum piety—the sin of the cave—is reflected powerfully in an interpretation of the eleventh-century biblical and Talmudic commentator Rashi (BT Shabbat 31a), to which I will devote a more extensive discussion in the next chapter. However, Rashi's interpretation bears mentioning here briefly as a concise illustration of how God Intoxication operates in the case of one of Jewish history's most influential figures.

The Talmud reports the story of a prospective convert who approaches Hillel the Elder with a strange request: "Make me a proselyte, on condition that you teach me the whole Torah while I stand on one foot." Rather than drive the man away (as did his counterpart Shammai), Hillel converts him on the spot, then says, "What is hateful to you, do not to your neighbor: that is the whole Torah. The rest is commentary; go and learn it.'" (BT Shabbat 31a)

Hillel's message seems straightforward: the core defining value of the Torah is to treat others ethically. For Rashi, however, Hillel's true meaning requires not only interpretation but radical reinterpretation. He therefore claims that "Neighbor refers to the Holy One, Blessed be He. Do not disobey His commandments, for it is hateful unto you when a friend disobeys yours." Rashi reverses the plain meaning of Hillel's maxim, erasing the ethical claim of the original and replacing it with a focus on God. Encountering this text, he seems to have been confronted with a profound theological quandary: Where is God in Hillel's calculation? How can you leave out God? Rashi cannot tolerate a definition of religious life whose essence is defined by how we treat others. More significant, he cannot see the fulfillment of moral responsibilities toward others as an expression of a relationship with God. His God-intoxicated theology makes it impossible for him to hear Hillel's words—so he changes them instead.

It is significant to note that Isaiah's stinging rebuke of those who seek God in prayer and ritual while ignoring their ethical responsibility to others (Isaiah 58, discussed in Chapter 1)—perhaps the tradition's most direct indictment of the so-called piety of God Intoxication—has itself become ritualized within the liturgy for Yom Kippur. On the day of the Jewish calendar when the dominant expression is immersion in prayer and ritual fasting, we read, "Is not this the fast that I have chosen: to loose the fetters of wickedness, to undo the bands of the yoke, and to let the oppressed go free, and that you break every yoke? Is it not to distribute your bread to the hungry, and bring the poor that are cast out to your house? When you see the naked, that you cover him, and that you hide not yourself from your own flesh?" (Isaiah 58:1–7)

There is a pointed irony to reading a critique of institutionalized ritual within an institutionalized framework—an irony that may have been the rabbis' motivation for including it in the liturgy in the first place. At the height of Jewish ritual fasting and prayer, they challenge the community to reflect critically on what we are doing in synagogue. Isaiah's message can be summarized in this way: Your prayer and fasting are worthless to me as long as there are hungry, poor, homeless, and naked people suffering just outside the walls of your religious sanctuary. Get out of synagogue and create a society of justice! There is a tragic irony in the realization that the Jewish community has taken the text that critiques the ritualization of the fast and instructs us to redefine piety and we have effectively neutralized its dominant message by treating it as another holiday reading, another prayer, another way of setting God, and not other people, before us at all times. God pronounces God's message, God's religious priorities, in the strongest terms, but we are too busy being consumed by God's presence even to hear God, much less to see others.

DIVINE MANIPULATION: PIOUS INDIFFERENCE AND THE GOD OF ABRAHAM

The second expression of monotheism's autoimmune disease can be found in the phenomenon I call God Manipulation. The great paradigm of God Manipulation is the myth of chosenness and the ways in which it is used to serve the self-interests of the anointed, to the exclusion of all others. The God-sanctioned indifference of God Manipulation is characterized not by subjecting our needs to God's will (God Intoxication) but by using God in the service of our own interests, while simultaneously waving the banner of divine approval. The notion of one God who is radically other creates a powerful fantasy of ownership in which the God of the universe is drafted into the service of one's local worldview. This self-interest under the pretense of piety makes God Manipulation such a difficult condition to detect, let alone counteract.

I remember when I became conscious of God Manipulation for the first time. It was in the summer of 1982, when as a young tank commander I found myself fighting for Israel in the first Lebanon War. My battalion, which was composed entirely of Orthodox yeshiva students, had spent the war battling the entrenched Syrian army along a mountainous path on the eastern side of Lebanon. My unit suffered devastating casualties, including my own tank, which was blown up, my driver seriously injured. When a temporary ceasefire was declared, we were the first unit to be replaced at the frontlines and were redeployed a number of miles back at the site of the picturesque Karoun Lake, where a tense battle had occurred a few days earlier. It was Friday afternoon, the sun was setting, and Shabbat was about to begin. We quickly parked and camouflaged our tanks. Soon, a deep sense of peace befell the unit as the Sabbath aura set in, and many traded their fire-retardant uniforms for white button-down shirts. For a moment, the filth, chaos, and horror of battle were lifted.

Finding ourselves in relative safety, we began to explore our immediate surroundings. To our surprise, we found the area littered with the corpses of numerous Syrian soldiers. The Israeli army has a standing policy of "no one left behind," dead or alive, and tremendous care and even sacrifice are expended to ensure that all of our dead receive the dignity of a proper burial. Upon encountering the bodies, I turned to the unit's chaplain, whose job it was to oversee the treatment of our unit's dead, and inquired about the possibility of organizing a burial detail for the fallen Syrian soldiers. To this day I remember the surprise I experienced at his dismissive response: "Does this really trouble you?" We don't need to care about them, was his clear message.

What would make a person, raised in a tradition that teaches that all human beings are created in the image of God, and that to be loyal to God means one should not remain indifferent, respond so indifferently? What was the cause of his blatant discrimination between Israeli and Syrian bodies—when as a rabbi he certainly was familiar with the law obligating us to care equally for the dead of non-Jews?

Granted, the heat of battle is not known as the ideal setting for moral sensitivity. But I have since come to understand that this response—"Does this really trouble you?"—was not merely a result of the pressure of war. It was the product of a religious sensibility rooted in a sense of being chosen and loved by God more: a love in the context of a zero-sum game, in which there is never enough to go around. God's love and care for me necessarily diminishes God's love and care for others. For this military chaplain, religious faith did not provide enough God to go around.

The Bible introduces this concept with the election of Abraham: "For I have singled him out." (Genesis 18:19) Prior to Abraham, all humanity, created in the image of God, was equal in God's eyes, benefiting from God's grace or suffering from God's wrath in accordance with their deeds. After God seemingly rejects Cain in favor of his brother Abel, God provides the basic moral logic that governs human-divine interaction. "And the Lord said to Cain, 'Why are you distressed, and why is your face fallen? Surely if you do right, there is uplift. But if you do not do right, sin crouches at your door.'" (Genesis 4:6–7)

With the call to Abraham, "Go forth . . . and I will make of you a great nation, and I will bless you, and I will make your name great" (Genesis 12:1–2), a new condition for receiving God's grace is put forth within monotheistic doctrine, a condition that has infected all monotheistic faiths hence. "I will bless those who bless you, and curse him who curses you. And through you all the families of the earth will be blessed." (Genesis 12:3) No longer is God the just judge of the whole earth but a biased judge who favors the elected ones, and treats others not merely in accordance with their merits (or demerits) but in relationship to what benefits the chosen.

This idea is put immediately into practice seven verses later, as the Bible tells the story of Abraham's descent into Egypt with his wife Sarah upon the outbreak of a famine in the land of Canaan. From the perspective of his future charge to do what is "just and right," Abraham's character throughout this episode is clearly less than exemplary, and certainly not up to the standards that were set forth as the grounds for his election. Knowing the dangers that he faces as a man married to a beautiful woman in a foreign land, he nevertheless leaves Canaan and secures his personal fate by convincing Sarah to declare herself unwed, and thus open to be taken by anyone with the power to do so. "If the Egyptians see you and think, 'She is my wife,' they will kill me and let you live. Please say that you are my sister, that it may go well with me because of you, and that I may remain alive thanks to you." (Genesis 12:12–13)

Despite Abraham's clearly poor behavior, when Pharaoh, unaware of her marital status, takes Sarah as a wife, it is he, and not Abraham, who is subjected to the divine wrath, while Abraham acquires great wealth, and both he and Sarah are saved. "And because of her, it went well with Abraham; he acquired sheep, oxen, asses, male and female slaves, she-oxes, and camels. But the Lord afflicted Pharaoh and his household with mighty plagues." (Genesis 12:16–17)

The lesson the Bible intends to emphasize is clear. Even if the chosen one is powerless and comes up against the greatest of human powers, as personified by Pharaoh; even if the chosen one is clearly wrong, and the nonchosen is blameless, the rule still applies: "I will bless those who bless you, and curse those who curse you." Through the principle of chosenness, the one God is removed from the transcendent stage and diminished into a national idol—with a particular twist. While in the world of idolatry each region or nation is affirmed through its own god, through the principle of chosenness, the universal God is drafted into the service of a particular worldview, leaving all others devoid of access to God's grace. This is the platform upon which divinely sanctioned indifference stands and the ground from which religiously endorsed injustice grows.

HOLY WAR AND THE SKEWED ETHICS OF CHOSENNESS

A potent example of religiously endorsed injustice can be found in the classic biblical treatment of the morality of war. "When you take the field against your enemies and see horses and chariots larger than yours, have no fear of them, for the Lord your God who brought you out of Egypt is with you." (Deuteronomy 20: 1) At first glance, this verse seems straightforward. Those who choose to be the enemies of Israel will also find themselves to be the enemies of God.

But who are these "enemies"? We might be inclined to read them as other nations who attack the Jewish people, threatening war and conquest. This self-defense reading makes sense in light of the invocation of the Exodus from Egypt. God's protection of the Jewish people in war extends the liberation from Egypt into an ongoing paradigm of divine protection: the God who fought for you against the evil Pharaoh and his army will also fight with you against any future Pharaoh you encounter.

Yet the Bible explicitly identifies the enemies in this passage not as aggressors but rather as victims of Jewish expansionary wars. "Thus you shall deal with all towns that lie very far from you, towns that do not belong to nations hereabout." (Deuteronomy 20:15) These enemies are not encountered in Israel, near Israel, or even far away—but "very far." The category of war described here is clearly not a defensive war against threatening neighbors but a war of expansion. Nevertheless, the Bible sanctions this war, places God on the side of Israel, and justifies the most horrific treatment of this "enemy":

> When you approach a town to attack it, you shall offer it terms of peace. And if it accepts your offer of peace, and opens to you, then it shall be that all the people who are found therein will become your tax-subjects, and will serve you. And if it will make no peace with you, but rather makes war against you, then you shall besiege it. And when the Lord your God delivers it into your hand, you shall smite every male thereof with the sword. And the women, and children, and cattle, and all that is in the city, including all of its spoils, you shall take for yourself as spoils. And you shall consume all the spoils of your enemy, which the Lord your God has given to you. (Deuteronomy 20: 10–14)

Through the disease of God Manipulation, the standards of justice are set aside, and the God who is supposed to be served through righteousness to all, and who is characterized as the judge of the whole earth, is suddenly transformed into a God who blinds people to their moral responsibility. All of Israel's wars are now defined as holy wars, sanctioned and sanctified by God. The chosen one's enemy is not limited to those who attack but expanded to include anyone who has something the chosen one desires. Conquest is not merely a vehicle of self-aggrandizement but through God Manipulation is converted into an expression of the Almighty's love. The God who redeemed the Children of Israel from the injustice of Pharaoh will remain by our side even as we join Pharaoh's ranks, expanding our empire through gratuitous wars of genocide, enslavement, pillaging, and general self-enrichment.

I characterize God Manipulation as an expression of religion's autoimmune disease because its effect is not merely to blind me to my moral responsibilities to others: ultimately, it blinds me also to myself and the person I have become. I cloak myself in the grace of God, whom I define as being with me regardless of what I do or deserve, attributing pious motivation and religious value to all of my behavior. Once we can no longer see who we have become, we have lost the ability to self-correct, to say I have sinned, and to repent. These are those who have lost their moral compass completely.

"HE FORFEITED THEIR MONEY TO ISRAEL": THE CYNICAL LOGIC OF GOD MANIPULATION

This blindness to our moral responsibility to others plagues all monotheistic faiths, and much of our treatment toward those we define as the nonchosen or nonenlightened follows a similar path. A troubling yet definitive example is found in the Talmud with regard to the status of the idolatrous non-Jew in civil claims. The *Mishneh* rules (Baba Kama 4:3) that when a Jew encounters an idolator in the public domain, the rules governing their responsibilities to each other are not symmetrical. Jews have no responsibility for any damage their animals cause others, while others have maximum responsibility for any such damage their animals cause to Jewish property.

The Talmud, which comments on the *Mishneh*, proceeds to justify this biased ruling in two ways, both of which are symptomatic of full-blown God Manipulation. In the first, the rabbis invoke a tradition that seven core commandments obligate all humanity ("the descendants of Noah"), and that for Jews these were superseded by the revelation of the Torah. "Rabbi Abahu thereupon said: 'He stood and measured the earth; He beheld and drove asunder the nations.' (Habakkuk 3:6) [This may be taken to imply that] God beheld the seven commandments which were accepted by all the descendants of Noah, but since they did not observe them, He rose up and forfeited their money to Israel." (BT Baba Kama 38a)

Setting aside for now the unilateral nature in which Jewish law determines that the non-Jewish world is obligated to a particular code and the presumption that its prescriptions "were accepted by the descendants of Noah," the seven Laws of Noah contain a prohibition against idolatry, obviously unheeded by the idolatrous nations.

The idolatrous world thus finds itself in direct violation of its supposed covenant with God, as defined unilaterally by rabbinic tradition. In the inexorable logic of God Manipulation, this standing transgression, an extension of an internal Jewish story, creates the self-evident grounds for divine sanction. As punishment, God abrogated the property rights of the non-Jews and turned their money over to the Jews. In this way, the rabbis close the circuit on a cynical rationalization of Jewish expropriation of non-Jewish property, which is recast as the noble implementation of God's will.

The second answer reflects an even more cynical form of God Manipulation. "Rabbi Johanan said that the same could be inferred from this [verse], 'He shined forth from Mount Paran [a reference to Mount Sinai and the revelation of the Torah],' [implying that] from Paran He forfeited their money to Israel." (Deuteronomy 32:2)

According to Rabbi Johanan, at Sinai, the moment when God and the Jewish people enter into a covenant grounded on the Torah, all those who do not partake in that covenant (non-Jews) have their property rights forfeited by God and given over to God's covenantal partner (Israel).

As this discussion so troublingly demonstrates, those who think they own God believe they have the right to determine whom God loves as well as the legal implications of that love. When chosenness permits the co-opting of God into the service of the interests of the chosen, the immoral becomes mysteriously moral, the profane miraculously holy. The infidel becomes not merely the subject of God's judgment but fair game for the believer. Forfeiting their claim to basic human needs, the outsiders have no rights; they are not seen. Most significant, the descent into craven self-interest becomes clothed in piety, as our manipulation of God makes us blind to our own moral corruption. Here we find God Manipulation, with its symptomatic self-blinding, in an advanced stage.

"POUR OUT YOUR WRATH": THE WARRIOR GOD OF ISRAEL

An analogous expression of God Manipulation finds its way into the most widely read book in Jewish tradition, the Haggadah of the Passover Seder. From a celebration of the victory of the enslaved and oppressed, the story swerves sharply into a narrative of messianic national triumphalism. After detailing the nature of Jewish slavery and the miraculous salvation of God, we are told to read, "Pour out Your wrath upon the nations that do not know You, upon the governments which do not call upon Your name. For they have devoured Jacob and desolated his home." (Psalm 79:6–7) "Pour out Your wrath on them; may Your blazing anger overtake them." (Psalm 69:25) The election of Israel, reflected in the Exodus story in the logic of the Haggadah, leads to co-opting God to destroy Israel's enemies.

Instead of praying for an Isaiah-like end of days in which all the nations on earth will "beat their swords into plowshares, and their spears into pruning hooks. Nation shall not take up sword against nation, and they shall never again teach war" (Isaiah 2:4), chosenness corrupts us into considering revenge an acceptable, even redemptive, aspiration.

God's vulnerability to manipulation unleashes the ideology that God is essentially a personal and national warrior for the Jewish people, who not only fights on our side against oppressors but also embraces wars of aggression to destroy all impediments to our national expansion. Because we are chosen, all acts taken to advance these interests become synonymous with God's will and immune to moral review.

MONOTHEISM'S LEGACY: A BLINDING INDIFFERENCE?

As this chapter has demonstrated, God Intoxication shuts down the vision of religious people, clearing the way for divinely sanctioned indifference to the needs, sensitivities, and interests of others, and indeed even of oneself. Since all pales in comparison to God, what could possibly be more important than demonstrating fidelity and loyalty to God's will, irrespective of the consequences or effects? This consuming vision of God eclipses not merely one's moral impulses but also one's awareness of, and regard for, the world. If the world is unimportant, moral responsibility to its inhabitants loses meaningful significance.

Instead of belittling and negating the significance of worldly concerns (including one's own), God Manipulation enables believers to justify unchecked self-interest. If Hillel obligates the Jewish faithful to place an ethical sensitivity to the other's needs at the top of our hierarchy of religious values, the myth of chosenness supports an image of God that subverts that very value, by enabling us to exclude most others from this obligation, legitimating a systemic moral double standard. For those who claim to own God, there is no sin that cannot be purified, sanctified, and ultimately transformed into a virtue.

These variations on monotheism's God-centered autoimmune disease are deeply entrenched. Are they an inherent part of the system, an unavoidable consequence and cost of religious life? If so, one must conclude that religion is destined to serve as a perpetual catalyst for moral mediocrity, corruption, and at times downright evil, self-defeated from fulfilling its aspiration to produce individuals and communities of moral excellence. Is this monotheism's enduring legacy to the world?

CHAPTER THREE

RECOVERING FROM GOD INTOXICATION

PROPHETIC FAILURE AND THE PRIMACY OF THE ETHICAL

God Intoxication, as we have learned, distorts monotheistic religion by defining religious piety exclusively in terms of immersion in God-centered ritual and consciousness. This consuming focus on a God who demands exclusive attention at all times and at all costs extracts a heavy price in the sphere of the ethical. God Intoxication devalues the human enterprise and consequently the significance of human ethical responsibility. How can religious people recover from this spiritual autoimmune disorder? How can we reclaim our monotheistic traditions so that they fulfill their intended roles as forces for good?

The prophets sharply critiqued the various manifestations of God Intoxication they encountered in their time. They insisted that religious devotion, without commensurate striving in the sphere of moral conduct, is a form of spiritual deviance and a perversion of the tradition's core values and goals. "I loathe, I spurn your festivals, I am not appeased by your solemn assemblies. If you offer me burnt offerings, or your meal offerings, I will not accept them; I will pay no heed to your gifts of fatlings. Spare Me the sound of your hymns, and let Me not hear the music of your lutes. But let justice well up like water, righteousness like an unfailing stream. Did you offer sacrifices and oblation to Me, those forty years in the wilderness, O house of Israel?" (Amos 5:21–25) Pointing to the intense covenantal intimacy of Israel and God's relationship with each other in the desert, the prophet Amos tries to redirect the core passion of a life with God to the moral treatment of others. In no period in Jewish history was God more present in the life of Israel but at the same time Judaism's ritual life so thin. Yet when we entered the land, and subsequently rebuilt the temple, we forgot the lesson of the desert and began to prioritize ritual over ethics. For the prophets, this is not merely a failure in memory but a core religious distortion. "Who asked this of you?" (Isaiah 1), Isaiah demands to know. The striving for closeness to God often seems in fact to cultivate a narcissistic illusion, a "slap in God's face," a false piety whose practitioners have strayed farther from God's intent than they could possibly imagine.

What the prophets failed to recognize—and why they ultimately failed in their mission to spur an ethical awakening among the Children of Israel—was precisely the "autoimmuneness" of the problem. Rather than seeing this misbehavior as arising from an internal contradiction within the tradition, they blamed errant human nature, the inclination to sin. Perhaps too closely identified with the God whose word they channeled, they did not grasp God's potentially wayward influence on the followers of revealed religion. In this sense, they perpetuate a divine misunderstanding of humanity. Nonetheless, their significance lies in their righteous call for the observance of the ethical and their sarcastic condemnation of all religious devotion that excludes it.

How can we perpetuate this prophetic message? One possibility acknowledges that Isaiah's goal of ethical reform requires a more comprehensive solution than restating its importance as a religious value. It requires rediscovering and reclaiming a religious system that does not merely attempt to balance love of God with love of neighbor but that clearly prioritizes love of neighbor over love of God. Healing God Intoxication begins by recognizing the religious primacy of the ethical. Not merely its legitimacy or its importance—but its primacy.

To recover from God Intoxication requires, in short, putting God second. For as long as devotion to God comes first, responsibility to other people—God's true purpose for humanity—will trail far, far behind.

"WHAT IS HATEFUL TO YOU": ASSERTING JUDAISM'S ETHICAL ESSENCE

Classical Jewish tradition's most prominent anti-God Intoxication figure is Hillel the Elder. The Talmud (BT Shabbat 31a) tells of a non-Jew who approaches Hillel's counterpart, Shammai, with a strange request: to be converted "while standing on one foot." Shammai, interpreting the request as a sign of insincerity and disrespect—I will convert as long as you can give me the Cliff Notes version—gruffly dismisses the prospective convert, stressing that at minimum he must recognize the seriousness that Jewish life entails.

The would-be convert, undeterred, approaches Hillel and repeats his request—and Hillel converts him on the spot. It is possible that Hillel hears the question in the same way as Shammai, but is simply willing to convert anyone, unconditionally, as a matter of policy. It is also possible, however, that Hillel understands the question differently. The request to learn all the Torah while standing on one foot may reflect a lack of sincerity, but also may reflect a serious question: I will convert, as long as you can tell me the essence of this tradition.

Judaism's hundreds of biblical commandments and thousands of rabbinic interpretations result in a sea of rules and norms in which it is easy for core religious priorities and goals to get lost. From this perspective, the convert's question reflects a legitimate spiritual desire to know the essential principles and values informing and animating the intricate structures of religious life. For without this essence, religion is just that, a set of empty structures devoid of any underlying meaning or truth.

Hillel's answer, in any event, provides the potential convert, and all subsequent rabbinic tradition, with an encapsulation of Judaism's core values. "What is hateful to you," Hillel states, "do not do to your neighbor: this is the whole Torah. The rest is commentary [upon this principle]; go and learn it." (BT Shabbat 31a)

This seemingly simple aphorism requires careful analysis. Hillel declares that the essential telos, or purpose, of Jewish tradition is not ritual or faith in God but rather a life defined by ethical sensitivity toward others. This priority of the ethical does not exclude ritual or devotional spirituality from the sphere of religious value and meaning, but it does make unequivocally clear that the tradition's overarching agenda is to regulate moral conduct, shaping individuals, and by extension communities, who place their treatment of others at the center of their religious lives.

"THE REST IS COMMENTARY": HILLEL'S ETHICAL LENS

"This is the whole Torah." On its surface, this proclamation might suggest that there is no spiritual dimension to the Jewish religious tradition, which does not care about a life with God that is expressed through ritual, prayer, and other devotional expressions of faith. We know, however, from myriad other stories cited in his name that Hillel considers these to be indispensable aspects of Jewish life. Referring to his dictum as "the whole Torah" is thus clearly not meant to be a descriptive statement but rather a statement of priority. He is responding, we will recall, to the convert's question "What is the essence?" That is, "I know there are a lot of details, but what is the underlying unity and purpose?"

Hillel's next remark, "the rest is commentary," helps to clarify the meaning of the declaration that precedes it. Judaism, Hillel states, cannot be reduced to ethical practices; but the whole system, ethical and ritual alike, must be governed by the highest ethical standards. "The rest is commentary" announces that while Judaism is not simply an ethical system, it is only to the extent that spiritual devotion is conducive to, and does not in any way undermine, a life of the ethical that it may find a legitimate place within the tradition. When the laws focused on cultivating devotion to God are understood to constitute a "commentary" to the laws defining moral behavior toward other human beings, the primacy of the ethical over what is conventionally understood as spiritual piety is established.

For someone whose religious value system is defined by Hillel's dictum, preventing a desecration of God's name could never outweigh the consequences such an act might have for the dignity of self and others. Just the opposite: only to the extent that moral responsibility to others is not merely considered as one factor in religious decision making, but adopted as the lens through which Jewish believers evaluate our religious practices, will the essence of the Torah be fulfilled. There is more to the Torah than ethics—"Go and learn it!"—but it must all be viewed through the lens of the ethical. Devotion to God can never undermine or override responsibility to others. As commentary, devotion embellishes but can never allow itself to transgress the ethical. Hillel takes religion off the path of God Intoxication and places it on a path toward moral excellence.

"GREAT IS THE RESPECT DUE OTHER HUMAN BEINGS"

This prioritization of the ethical in which all the rest of Torah is commentary finds powerful expression in two legal rulings cited in the name of the famous Babylonian Talmudic scholar Rava. Both cases involve dilemmas of priority, in which a person is

faced with the requirement to perform two commandments—
one with an ethical underpinning, the other focusing on faith—
but because of limited resources is only able to perform one.
Before exploring the details of these dilemmas, we should note
that the ultimate subject of the discussion—what takes precedence?—speaks directly to Hillel's response to the convert. It is
not enough simply to declare the importance of the ethical, for
God Intoxication has the power to deafen us to this message (for
example, see Rashi's [re]interpretation of Hillel's maxim discussed in the previous chapter). To fulfill the promise of Hillel's
declaration, the ethical must be integrated into our everyday
lives by way of binding communal norms. The ethical becomes
primary when it is established as the overriding value that guides
the formulation of these norms.

The first case takes place on a Friday night (the Sabbath)
during the holiday of Hanukah, when both the Sabbath and
Hanukah candles require lighting. The lighting of Hanukah candles commemorates God's miraculous hand in transforming one
can of oil, sufficient for one day only, into oil sufficient for eight
days, which enabled the purification and reconsecration of the
temple in Jerusalem. The Sabbath candles are lit in the home
on Friday evening in order to bring light, joy, and happiness
into the home on the Sabbath. However, in a world of limited
resources, there is not always enough money for both. What if,
Rava poses, a person only has enough money for either Sabbath
or Hanukah candles? Which takes precedence?

In the second case, the limited resource is not money but
time. In this case, it is the holiday of Purim, on which the Jewish
people celebrate God's assistance in redeeming us from the evil
hands of the anti-Semitic Haman, who strove to kill all the Jews
in the kingdom of ancient Persia. The event and God's miracle
are commemorated through the reading of the book of Esther.
What, Rava poses, should one do if, on the way to synagogue
to read the book of Esther, one is called upon to participate in

the duty of burying a member of the community? Here too, the underlying question is, What takes precedence? What are Judaism's priorities?

Now let us explore Rava's two cases, each of which is presented as a choice between mutually exclusive options. In terms of their meaning, both the lighting of Hanukah candles and the reading of the book of Esther are categorized by the Talmudic rabbis as forms of "publicizing the miracle" (*pirsuma nisa*), symbolic acts pointing to the miraculous hand of God at work in Jewish history. This commandment to publicize God's miraculous assistance was deemed fitting and necessary with respect to the holidays of Hanukah and Purim because the miraculous nature of these events is not self-evident to readers of the historical record. Unlike the biblical story of Passover—which includes no requirement of "publicizing the miracle"—neither of these postbiblical stories involves the most classical or archetypal sign of miraculous intervention, the overturning of nature. In Passover, God's redeeming hand is the crux of the story from beginning to end.

The book of Maccabees, however, our closest historical source for the Hanukah tale, tells not of a protective God breaking into history to defeat the Hellenizing Greeks and their Jewish collaborators but rather of the zealous and courageous Maccabees. In the book of Esther, God is never mentioned. The Jewish people appear to have been saved by the integrity, ingenuity, and fearlessness of Esther and Mordekhai.

By foregrounding the tradition about the single canister of oil lasting for eight days, and translating that tradition into the candle-lighting ritual that would become synonymous with the holiday, the rabbis shifted the meaning of Hanukah from a military victory in which the Hasmoneans prevail to a spiritual victory in which God prevails.

Similarly, by enveloping the book of Esther within a communal religious ritual, framed by blessings that describe the salvation of God, the rabbis added a dimension of divine significance that was not obvious from a simple reading of history. In the postbiblical era, whether in exile in Persia or even in the land of Israel, when the great powers of history are the Assyrians, Persians, Greeks, and Romans, it is our responsibility to seek out and give voice to God's redeeming presence in our lives. These commemorative acts of publicizing miracles create an awareness of a God who is present for us in our journey through history even if often in hidden and mysterious ways. In a certain sense, through Hanukah and Purim, the tradition prompts the Jewish people to see God where they otherwise might not, countering the inclination to remain indifferent to God's integral role in human life when not accompanied by miraculous intervention.

It is against the background of these rituals, which enable the Jewish people to see a God whom they do not normally see, that the rabbis ask: What happens when that opportunity conflicts with one's obligations to family and others? In contrast with Hanukah candles, intended to help us more clearly see God, the lighting of Shabbat candles is derived from the obligation to "declare Shabbat a joy" (Isaiah 58:13) and classified by the tradition as *ner beito*—"a light for the family." If forced to prioritize one of these types of light over the other, which do we choose? Do we create joy in our home by lighting a candle that enables us to see our family? Or do we light a candle that helps us to see God more clearly? Do we read the book of Esther to see the hidden hand of God in Jewish history? Or do we pay respect to a recently departed human being awaiting burial, exposed and helpless until we lend our own assisting hands?

Following the spirit of Hillel's principle, Rava rules in both cases that Jewish tradition prioritizes seeing human needs and concerns over seeing and publicizing God's presence. When we must choose, we choose Sabbath candles, "on account of the importance of the peace within the home [*Shalom bayit*] that it enables." (BT Shabbat 23b) When we must choose, we choose human dignity and bury the dead: "Great is the respect due to other human beings [*kavod ha-bri'ot*] for it overrides the fulfillment of any negative commandment within the Torah." (BT Megillah 3b)

"DO THAT WHICH IS RIGHT AND GOOD": BEYOND THE LAW

The primacy of the ethical enshrined in Hillel's maxim is further developed within Jewish tradition through the principle of "beyond the requirement of the law" (*lifnim mishurat ha-din*). If Rava draws upon the spirit of Hillel to assert that, in cases where ethical and God-centered imperatives conflict, the ethical takes precedence, "beyond the requirement of the law" (henceforth "beyond") can prompt us to be guided by the ethical in those areas the law does not cover. It also establishes a standard with the capacity to critique and correct existing laws that do not reflect the primacy of the ethical. For the challenge of the ethical in Jewish tradition is not limited to moments of priority; it also includes areas in which the tradition itself fails to live up to the standard set by Hillel.

These two aspects of "beyond" are articulated within Jewish tradition by two of the most important medieval rabbinic legalists and philosophers, Nachmanides and Maimonides. Nachmanides, commenting on the biblical verse, "And you shall do that which is right and good within the sight of God" (Deuteronomy 6:18), asks, "Is this not a superfluous commandment?" The Bible spends hundreds of chapters outlining hundreds of particular positive and negative obligations. Thus, isn't "doing what is right and good" already covered—isn't it constituted by striving to perform them? What is the need for such a vague, overarching commandment or, for that matter, any commandment beyond fulfilling the mitzvot revealed by God at Sinai?

Nachmanides begins by acknowledging that in "line with the plain meaning of scripture, the verse means, 'Keep the commandments of God.'" One way of understanding this verse is simply as a summary of religious life and not as an independent commandment at all. But then he proceeds to offer an alternative approach:

> Our rabbis have a beautiful commentary on this verse. They have said: "That which is right and good refers to compromise and going beyond the requirement of the letter of the law." The intent of this is as follows: At first Moses stated you are to keep His statutes and His testimonies which He commanded you, and now He is stating that even where He has not commanded you, give thought, as well, to do what is good and right in His eyes, for He loves the good and the right. Now this is a great principle, for it is impossible to mention in the Torah all aspects of man's conduct with his neighbors and friends, and all his various transactions, and the ordinances of all societies and countries. But since He mentioned many of them . . . He reverted to state in a general way that, in all matters, one should do what is good and right, including even compromise and going beyond the requirements of the law. . . . Thus [a person must seek to refine his behavior] in every form of activity, until he is worthy of being called "good and upright."

Nachmanides argues that the commandment to "do that which is right and good within the sight of the Lord" is a response to an inherent limitation of any legal system: the impossibility of addressing every possible case. No legal system can exhaust every instance, every dilemma that a person will face within the course of his or her life. How do we approach such moments? For Nachmanides, as for Rava and Hillel before him, the answer is to be guided by the desire to become "worthy of being called 'good and upright.'" This serves as the organizing principle for decision making in moments in which the Torah does not offer clear direction. By articulating the system's essence, Nachmanides, in the tradition of Hillel, gives it a new, ever-expanding voice that speaks beyond the scope of what is covered by its present incarnation. For Nachmanides, then, "beyond" is precisely Hillel's essence broadly applied, the guiding principle for building a tradition in which the ethical continues to be primary.

"THE QUALITY OF PIETY AND THE WAY OF WISDOM": CORRECTING THE LAW

Nachmanides's assumption is that where the tradition does have a voice, it will obviously live up to the standard of what is just and right. However, as we have seen, the autoimmune disease of God Intoxication distorts the religious vision both of individuals who speak in the name of God and of the tradition itself. Whether it is Abraham willing to sacrifice his son in the name of God or Talmudic rabbis willing to strip people in the marketplace and shame them so as not to desecrate God's name, neither of these seems to meet the standard of what is just and right.

Thus, Nachmanides's assumption about a baseline of justice and righteousness within the tradition is not necessarily self-evident—and here Maimonides takes Hillel's principle a step further. Commenting on the biblical permissibility to "work an idolatrous slave with rigor," Maimonides explains that in the framework of the Bible, the rights of the idolatrous slave are in fact quite limited; according to the letter of the law, it is permitted to demand extreme and difficult work. Indeed, the Hebrew word used here for "rigor" (*be-farekh*) is the same word used to describe the way Pharaoh and his taskmasters treated Israelite slaves in Egypt. When the roles are reversed, and Jews are in possession of heathen slaves, the Bible allows us to treat them the way Pharaoh treated us.

And yet, after acknowledging the fact of the biblical law, Maimonides adds, "Though such is the rule, it is the quality of piety and the way of wisdom that a man be merciful and pursue justice and not make his yoke heavy upon the slave or distress him." (Maimonides, *Mishneh Torah*, Hilkhot Avadim 9:1) Maimonides here introduces a different notion of "beyond the requirement of the law": "The quality of piety and the way of wisdom." The radical nature of this statement lies in its clear implication that these qualities are not necessarily found within the law itself. According to Maimonides, Hillel's core principle is an aspiration that the current legal system does not always fulfill. The Jewish people were formed under conditions of slavery, and much of the Torah is framed explicitly as a response to this experience. How can we then allow ourselves to violate this founding principle and to enshrine this violation within the legal tradition itself? While acknowledging the scriptural law, Maimonides invokes the principle of the primacy of the ethical—of "beyond"—to create a sphere of spiritual aspiration for moral excellence that transcends the current state of the law.

To strive for wisdom and piety, to meet the standard of Hillel and fulfill the raison d'etre of Jewish tradition, requires a willingness to go "beyond." This claim may seem surprising and counterintuitive: shouldn't observing the law be enough? The difficulty lies mainly in that the law comes with the mantle of divine legitimacy and authority, and thus can easily be mistaken as an end in itself. What could motivate a person to strive to go beyond it?

It is one thing to invoke the metalegal principle of "beyond" to resolve situations where two obligations conflict; it is another to invoke it to fill in places where the law is silent. And it is yet another thing still to recognize that the tradition itself is flawed and in need of repair, that it permits immoral behavior, practices of the impious and unwise. The tradition thus faces a difficult educational challenge, for it is not sufficient merely to declare the primacy of the ethical, which is difficult to assimilate in light of prevailing religious assumptions and norms. The educational system must be geared to cultivate people committed to the standard of the pious, the wise, the just, and the right, and who insist that the tradition live up to this standard as well.

"MERCIFUL PEOPLE WHO HAVE MERCY UPON ALL": JEWISH ETHICAL IDENTITY

The arguments Maimonides employs, in his attempt to cultivate the religious personality for which Hillel yearned, merit closer examination. He continues, "Cruelty and effrontery are not frequent except with heathen who worship idols. The children of our father Abraham, however, i.e., the Israelites, upon whom the Holy One, blessed be He, bestowed the favor of the Law and laid upon them statutes and judgments, are merciful people who have mercy upon all." (Maimonides, *Mishneh Torah*, Hilkhot Avadim 9:1)

Here, in a formulation very much in the spirit of Hillel, Maimonides states explicitly what he considers to be the defining characteristic of Jewish identity. If Hillel declares the essence of Judaism, Maimonides declares the essence of what it means to be a Jew. In a seeming paradox, he argues that those who merely follow the law will become something different from a Child of Abraham, straying from the core of the ancestral identity.

On the question of how such moral lapses made their way into the sacred legal code in the first place, Maimonides is here silent. (How Maimonides explains this issue of biblical moral lapses will be discussed at length in chapter 5.) For the purposes of the current analysis, however, what is most significant is his refusal to allow what is written to set the moral standard by which Jews must abide. To the contrary, the ethical for Maimonides constitutes the standard against which the law must be judged and, if necessary, corrected. Otherwise, we end up placing ourselves, in certain instances, in the more disturbingly paradoxical situation of undermining our identities as Jews by following the law. And this is precisely Maimonides's point: one is in fact less Jewish when following the law than when going beyond what it requires. Indeed, to merit the name "Children of Abraham," we must in essence make going beyond the requirement of the law the ultimate law, the normative value system that guides how we process and transform the legal system we inherit. For it is only in the sphere of "beyond" that one can find the most complete expression of one's identity as a Jew.

Maimonides, however, takes his lesson about the primacy of the ethical as expressed in the concept of "beyond" one step further: "Thus also it is declared by the attributes of the Holy One, blessed be He, which we are enjoined to imitate: 'And his mercies are over all his works.'" (Psalm 145:9) Since God is merciful over all God's works, we must strive to be merciful as well. To stray from the path of wisdom and piety is thus not only to disconnect oneself from the essence of Jewish identity but also to distance oneself from God.

"BECAUSE THEY FOLLOWED THE LAW": THE LEGAL DUTY TO GO BEYOND

"Beyond" thus pushes those who follow the tradition not to feel religiously satisfied by merely doing what is written, creating a space for the ethical in instances where the law itself fails. In doing so, it demands a redefinition of what constitutes the law, which must ultimately be understood as living in accordance with the path of piety and wisdom and being merciful upon all. Those dimensions of inherited law that fail to give sufficient expression to this principle must be recognized and corrected. Maimonides, then, strongly reinforces the imperative not merely to state the importance of the ethical but also to create an alternative God-language in which God accepts—indeed, demands—a seemingly secondary role within the religious system.

This transformation of "beyond the law" into the essence of the law itself is poignantly expressed in a Talmudic passage that discusses the reasons the Second Temple was destroyed and the

Jewish people sent into exile. The Talmud first suggests that the temple's destruction was "because the Jewish people followed the law," but quickly amends this suggestion to divest it of its heretical antinomianism—while remaining theologically radical. "Rather," the Talmud claims, "Jerusalem was destroyed because they only followed the law, and did not go beyond it." (BT Baba Metzia 30b)

According to this passage, going "beyond" the letter of the law is not optional but a normative duty: God refuses to reside in our midst as long as we are a community that "only" follows the law. If the consequence of following the law is to disconnect us from the essence of the Torah, Jewish identity, and Jewish community, then the distinction between "the law" and "beyond the law" becomes meaningless and the primacy of the ethical takes its rightful place as the defining Jewish obligation.

"GO AND RETURN IT": A CASE STUDY IN "BEYOND"

This radical Maimonidean vision of "beyond" finds a heroic Talmudic exemplar in Rabbi Shimon ben Shetah. (JT Baba Metzia 2:5) In antiquity, rabbis were prohibited from receiving financial compensation for performing their rabbinical duties, and Shimon ben Shetah made his living in the cotton trade. In one story, his students plead with him for permission to buy him a donkey, to make his labor less burdensome and more efficient, freeing up more time for him to teach Torah. Finally they make the purchase, and after examining the donkey they discover a precious stone. They report the news to their beloved teacher, reveling in the good fortune that he would never have to labor again. They are celebrating what they readily interpret as a miracle, a kind of divine communication suggesting a clear future course for Shimon ben Shetah. With this miracle, they presume, God has revealed God's plan for him to spend more time teaching his students. After all, from the perspective of Jewish law (*halakhah*), he was under no obligation to return what he had found, for under *halakhah*, when a Jew finds an object lost by an idolatrous gentile, there is no legal responsibility to return it. Protected under the law, Shimon ben Shetah would appear to have been free to embrace the new lifestyle afforded by the found jewel.

Instead, he deflates the celebration with a simple question: Is the owner aware that one of his precious stones was connected to the donkey? The students answer that he was not. "Then go and return it," he instructs them. Later Talmudic editors question Shimon ben Shetah's stance, for the law is clear that there is no legal obligation to return an idolater's lost property.

But the text does not present Shimon ben Shetah as facing even a minimal dilemma. He knows what is ethical—notwithstanding either the revelation of a personal "miracle" or the rabbinic interpretation of Jewish law. This stance represents a powerful perspective: the ethical good, the "beyond the law," is a sphere of obligation that is primary to the law.

To build a religious tradition around the primacy of the ethical is critical to overcoming the God Intoxication that plagues and subverts the spiritual priority of human moral responsibility. The primacy of the ethical must be expressed in its role as the guiding mechanism for resolving legal conflicts, for stepping in where law is silent, and serving as a corrective where the law itself fails to live up to the standards that comprise the essence of Jewish tradition, identity, and community.

"WHAT DO PEOPLE SAY ABOUT HIM?": HUMAN ETHICS AND GOD'S REPUTATION

It might be tempting to interpret Hillel's prioritization of the ethical as creating a dichotomy between a humanistic and a theocentric religious life—relegating not only ritual but also God to a secondary role. In this reading, it is precisely the dichotomy that curbs our tendency toward God Intoxication. By remembering that the ultimate telos of Jewish tradition is to regulate how people treat each other, we work to ensure that people do not become intoxicated with religious passion.

But another source within Jewish tradition offers a conceptual framework for preventing God Intoxication without need for such a dichotomous opposition. In a sense, it might be seen as an attempt to answer the critique of Hillel implicit in Rashi's radical reinterpretation of his maxim. We can hear Rashi crying out—Hillel, you forgot about God!—leading him to divest Hillel's imperative of its ethical content and transforming it into a call to fulfill God's mitzvot.

In the Talmudic tradition, every sin a person commits is ultimately atoneable. Whether through repentance, various forms of punishment, or the metaphysical machinations of Yom Kippur, the Day of Atonement, the sinner is given a second chance. With this rule, however, the Talmud offers one exception: a sin for which there is, in this life, no forgiveness; a single act that makes achieving realignment with God impossible. For the sin of desecrating or profaning God's name (*hillul Hashem*), atonement can only be achieved through death. (BT Yoma 86a)

If Jewish tradition considers this to be the most heinous form of human deviance, we benefit from paying close attention to how it is defined. What constitutes the desecration or profanation of God's name? The Talmud offers an extremely surprising response: "Rav said: 'If, for example, I [that is, someone like me, a rabbi] take meat from the butcher, and do not pay him at once.'" According to this definition, God's name is desecrated when a rabbi is perceived to be using his status to create a financial advantage for himself—in this case, using the butcher's possible inhibition to ask for payment to curry special treatment.

Rav's response is not what we expect. One would imagine the desecration or profanation of God's name to be associated with acts like cursing or blaspheming God, using God's name inappropriately, or treating something that has been consecrated to God with disrespect. Rav declares that the core desecration occurs when those most closely associated with God act in ways that would be perfectly legitimate for other people but cannot pertain to them. Many people go to a butcher and ask to pay tomorrow, or next week, or next month. The rabbi, however, according to Rav, must abide by a higher standard than others. For if a "regular" individual (one who is not a rabbi) acts inappropriately, this behavior reflects only on him or her. But the rabbi, perceived to be a carrier of God's name, who is uniquely responsible for embodying the positive impact of living a godly life, thus also holds a unique ability to profane it.

Rav's definition of *hillul Hashem* represents a significant departure from the strain of Talmudic thinking discussed in the previous chapter, which holds that nothing is more important than God's commandment, no matter how trivial the commandment may seem. (BT Berakhot 19b) Rav argues, in essence, that the God of Judaism is a God who has chosen to live within this world; a God who, to quote Rabbi Abraham Joshua Heschel, is ever "in search of man," desiring to be known and loved by the human beings who populate God's world.

It seems reasonable to step back and ask, how is it possible to desecrate God's name? Is God not transcendent and thus immune from desecration? The key to approaching this question lies in recognizing that the term *desecration* here refers not to God but to the name of God. The God of Judaism wants a name, a reputation among God's creation. The God who creates a world populated by human beings, who plants a garden and gives the Torah, is a God who is actively involved in human history, a God who desires to be not just of assistance but also of importance to humanity.

Under the distorting influence of God Intoxication, however, the desire to sanctify God is translated into a consuming prioritization of devotion to God and corresponding sacrifice of the ethical. Rav steps in to correct this misconception. Sanctifying God's name is indeed Judaism's central mission, but

God Intoxication misunderstands sanctification. Indeed, it is a misunderstanding of the nature of the reputation God seeks to cultivate among humanity in this world.

The God who seeks a good name, who yearns to be known, loved, respected, and worshiped, places the power for both sanctification and desecration of the Divine Name in the hands of those from whom God seeks affirmation. The commandment to sanctify God's name, and to avoid its desecration, requires that the religious person not think about what he or she believes God may want but rather about what people want; to ask, in other words, what ordinary individuals respect about and consequently expect from God. Thus, the most theocentric of commandments is reshaped through the insight of Rav into the most anthropocentric of commandments, one in which a God-centered consciousness requires a shift to a human-centered consciousness by virtue of God's own stated priority; which is precisely to claim the recognition that comes from a good name.

What engenders disrespect in the eyes of ordinary people? Rav argues that the most significant factor is how one treats others and uses religion either to motivate or to excuse oneself from common decent behavior. People value moral decency and dismiss dishonesty. Consequently, God's name and reputation are intimately connected to the level of moral decency of those who are perceived to be God's representatives or followers. What follows is a true passion for sanctifying God's name that cannot remove us from the ethical but rather must move us toward it, keeping our vision trained with ever more focus on our relationships with, and treatment of, others—for this is what ultimately exerts the most impact upon people's sense of God. It is as if Rav were responding to Rashi: You are misreading Hillel. You think he has set up a dichotomy between love of human beings and love of God, and you have taken up the opposing side. But this is a false dichotomy, and not what Hillel intended. God, having chosen to live in this world, by implication has also chosen how

God's name is to be sanctified. The ultimate medium through which human beings assess a godly quality is in the ethical treatment of others.

For Rav, the remedy to God Intoxication is not a focus on ethics that excludes or even devalues religious passion. The purpose of divine commandments, after all, is not merely to regulate how human beings treat each other. Rather, they constitute a reflection of God's love and concern for human life, a desire to be a partner with humanity in the unfolding of our journey and story.

When representatives of God appear to act in ways that do not adhere to the highest moral standard, their behavior reflects poorly on God, and consequently, God's name is desecrated. The inverse is also true. God's name is sanctified when God's representatives—rabbis, who also serve as aspirational models for general Jewish behavior—place ethical sensitivity and responsibility at the center of their lives, and by extension, at the center of Jewish identity. Thus, Rav's redefinition of spiritual piety within the context of moral striving is taken further in the continuation of this Talmudic passage: "Abaye explained: As it was taught: 'And you shall love the Lord your God,' which means that the Name of Heaven be beloved because of you." (BT Yoma 86b) In the Bible, God's presence is mediated primarily first through the tabernacle, and then later through the temple. Here the rabbinic tradition declares that in the evolution of Jewish history God's presence is no longer mediated through a place at all but through the moral integrity of God's representatives as they walk through the world. Their treatment of others is an expression of their love of God—and by extension, their reputation is God's reputation.

> If someone studies Scripture and Mishnah, and attends on the disciples of the wise, is honest in business, and speaks pleasantly to persons, what do people then say concerning him? "Happy the father who taught him Torah, happy the

teacher who taught him Torah; woe unto people who have not studied the Torah; for this man has studied the Torah: Look how fine his ways are, how righteous his deeds! Of him does Scripture say: "And He said unto me: Thou art My servant, Israel, in whom I will be glorified." But if someone studies Scripture and Mishnah, attends on the disciples of the wise, but is dishonest in business, and discourteous in his relations with people, what do people say about him? "Woe unto him who studied the Torah, woe unto his father who taught him Torah; woe unto his teacher who taught him Torah!" This man studied the Torah: Look, how corrupt are his deeds, how ugly his ways; of him Scripture says: In that men said of them, "These are the people of the Lord, and are gone forth out of His land." (BT Yoma 86b)

Yearning for closeness with God does not translate into leaving the world like Shimon bar Yokhai and his son. Loving God does not mean sacrificing one's humanity but creating a human world in which God's name is beloved through acts of kindness and decency, by treating others how we would want to be treated, which is how God would want us to treat them.

ETHICS VERSUS FAITH: A FALSE CHOICE

Perhaps one of the greatest risk factors for the autoimmune disorder of God Intoxication is an adherence to the false dichotomy that we often construct between God and humanity, between faith and ethics. When perceived as an either-or question between people and God, how could I not choose God? In this distorted religious discourse, the ethical becomes identified with the secular, in direct opposition to the religious. Religious people often respond to this perception of a zero-sum game by retreating into a defensive posture, seeking ways to express their disdain for ethics and prove that their devotion to God far exceeds such "secular" concerns as other people's vulnerabilities and needs. In this acute form of God Intoxication, any gesture toward the ethical is perceived as indifference to God. What Rav and Abaye teach is that the idea that we come close to God through acts of transcendence is simply wrong. We come close to God by putting God second, precisely as God has commanded us to do. Thus, truly to walk with God is to walk with human beings through all of our shared struggles and needs. When the ethical becomes the primary sphere of Jewish spiritual striving and the dominant focus of our religious culture, theology, and practice, we create a space for the divine to rest within our communities.

What these sources illuminate, then, is a rejection of the perceived split that is rooted in the dichotomy between the physical and the spiritual. What emerges instead is a Jewish narrative of a God who embraces history and humanity, recognizing that the God of creation is not a contradiction of God's perfection. For how could a perfect God be implicated in something so imperfect?

Why God chooses to participate in and care about the story of humanity is a mystery Jewish tradition never fully answers. But the mystery does not undermine the reality of this God, whose name is not desecrated when a person finds him- or herself in clothing of mixed fabrics while walking in the street and fails to immediately strip it off. It is desecrated, rather, by the religious attitude that honors the commandment of mixed kinds (*kilayim*) over human dignity. It is desecrated when we fail to remember that to love God is to make God beloved to others by virtue of our moral example. God is not in competition with the ethical, for God desires the ethical above all else. In this light, religious passion is transformed from a destructive symptom of religion's autoimmune disease into a fuel for moral greatness. Only when we internalize the message of Hillel's maxim will God's presence find a home among humanity. Only then will we create the human society for which God yearns.

CHAPTER FOUR

IMMUNIZING AGAINST GOD MANIPULATION

"BECAUSE IT IS GOOD"

As I discussed in chapter 2, a primary cause of the spiritual autoimmune disease that can plague monotheistic religions comes directly from the potential for God and religion to be manipulated in a way that quiets the voices of moral conscience, draping self-interest in a cloak of pious devotion and stripping those defined as "other" of moral status. God Manipulation, the condition that sanctions such self-interest with the stamp of divine and religious approval, has proven a pervasive and perilous symptom of monotheism throughout the history of human social life. To protect humanity from this perversion of God's image, and to immunize religion from itself, is an existential need of the utmost urgency.

Any serious attempt at a theological remedy to God Manipulation must begin by affirming not only the primacy of the good but also its autonomy, or independence, from the claims of faith. To paraphrase the famous passage in the Platonic dialogue *Euthyphro*, Socrates asks whether something is loved by the gods because it is good, or is it good because it is loved by the gods? For something to be loved by the gods because it is good means that religion does not determine the good, and thus must itself adhere to the standards of a good that is defined externally—or be judged as morally lacking. For something to be good because it is loved by the gods means that whatever the gods love is by definition good, for what constitutes the good is fixed by their will—with no external moral check on divine preference. Socrates ultimately posits that the gods love the thing because it is good, which is another way of positing the autonomy of the ethical.

Only when this autonomy is established and embraced will monotheistic religion become immune from God Manipulation. Only when religious people can point to a standard of right and good and just, grounded in an independent moral conscience, can we prevent the systemic, pseudo-pious violation of basic morality toward others that has been such a prominent and persistent feature of religious life.

When the ethical is autonomous, God cannot sanction indifference toward those deemed not to have been "chosen," for moral duty to the other both precedes and supersedes any tradition that might appear to sanction such discrimination. It severely limits the ability of religion to define (and continually redefine) the standards of the good in self-interested, self-aggrandizing ways. When religion no longer has (or indeed makes any claim to) the authority to determine the good, all religious doctrine must adhere to autonomous ethical standards. No exceptions, exemptions, or loopholes in the name of God can ever apply.

THE POSSIBILITY OF MORAL KNOWLEDGE

Before making the argument for the autonomy of the ethical within Jewish tradition, it is worthwhile to elaborate what I mean by an autonomous moral good. One may argue that God loves the good because it is good, but can humans determine, much less know, what the good is on their own?

While some, most notably Thomas Hobbes in his book *Leviathan*, believe that the good is of "uncertain signification" ("for one calleth wisdom, what another calleth fear; and one cruelty what another justice"), and that humans are not motivated by the good but rather by a primal understanding and connection to self-interest, the history of moral philosophical discourse is by and large grounded on the assumption that humans are capable—whether by proper education (Aristotle, *Nicomachean Ethics*) or inherent constitution (Kant, *Grounding for the Metaphysics of Morals*)—of knowing the good. Whether God invests us with these capabilities when creating us in the divine image, or whether they are innately embedded in our human reason, compassion, or conscience, these capabilities endow human beings with the intrinsic capacity to discern the good.

Our everyday social life presupposes this same assumption. As Michael Walzer argues in *Just and Unjust Wars*, our experiences of moral disappointment, judgment, outrage, not to speak of the willingness to impose punishment, are all animated by the unspoken premises that we know what morality means, that our morality is shared and stable, and that our fellow human being knows or is capable of having known the good and ought to have lived accordingly (with the failure to do so constituting the understandable cause of our negative feelings and judgment, as per P. F. Strawson in *Freedom and Resentment*). It is not a failure to have read the correct sacred scripture that leads to this verdict, but a failure to access one's essentially human nature.

It is important to emphasize that these assessments of human aptitude do not assume that we are endowed with an innate ability or inclination to do the good, but merely to know it. A variety of factors—self-interest, evil inclinations, and, as I have argued, religious commitments and ideology—can sway us from doing the good and paint human history with the careless brush of moral mediocrity. But these failures neither impinge on the claim to the knowledge itself nor bear witness against it.

THE CHALLENGE OF HUMAN SUBJECTIVITY

A primary criticism of this assumption regarding the existence of an innate human capacity to know the good is the fluctuation and multiplicity of moral positions over time and among people and societies. If we indeed know the good, how can we explain the profound diversity and disagreements regarding the content of that which we purportedly know? The sense of moral uncertainty to which this phenomenon gives rise is one of the perennial selling points of religion, which purports to offer salvation from the mess of moral uncertainty. Religion promises to redeem us, here and now, from having to claim that we *know*—from the false expectation that we discern for ourselves, and by ourselves, what constitutes the good. It supplies us, as it were, with the antidote to human ignorance: a divinely ordained permanent and universal program for our moral life that transcends time, space, cultures, and societies.

The moral comfort that religion provides is existentially profound. The angst that a human-based morality leads not only to moral uncertainty but also to the chaos of moral relativism is so deep that the claim for the autonomy of the good often falls on deaf ears.

Let's alleviate some of the fear. It is interesting to notice that despite the significant moral disagreements that typify human society, we do not in fact live in a morally chaotic and relativistic universe. While moral disagreements abound, the vast majority of our differences pertain to the application of core moral principles or to their implementation, and rarely to the principles themselves. Many of these principles, such as the value of human life, concern for others, prohibition on violence, and the minimizing of suffering and harm, have remained remarkably consistent over time and social context (see H. L. A. Hart, *The Concept of Law*, and Michael Walzer, *Interpretation and Social Criticism*). When they are found to be absent, it is not viewed as evidence of their moral subjectivity but rather of moral failure on the part of those who are not committed to them.

Because human society shares universal moral principles, however, does not mean that we have a universal code of ethics. We may agree about the principles but find ourselves in disagreement over what weight to give to competing values when they conflict. In addition, what constitutes the good life, successful life, or happiness; who counts as fully human; who counts as virtuous; to whom must one show concern; who is entitled to political power and how and when—it is here that we disagree, and must inevitably disagree, as our varying needs and religious and cultural sensibilities are brought into the equation. The disagreements are in the application and rarely in the core principles themselves (see Michael Walzer, *Spheres of Justice*).

The critical point to acknowledge, however, is that this disagreement over application is not in any event the inheritance of autonomous "secular," human-based morality alone but plagues divine-based ethical systems as well. Not only do different divinely ordained systems disagree over the application of these principles, but even within one particular religious tradition, there is never a monolithic answer to the questions of application. A life with God does not create moral consistency across cultures and societies but itself is the grounds for this inconsistency, as each claims that God meant "this" and not "that." Regardless of the origin of our moral knowledge, difference is a universal and permanent feature of human institutions.

The inability of religion to save us from ourselves is even more foundational. The moment "the word" is given, it comes under the control of human interpreters, who assign to it diverse meanings. Revelation inherently involves what Hans-Georg Gadamer calls a "fusion of horizons" (*Truth and Method*), as the revealed word and those to whom it is revealed necessarily combine in assigning its content and meaning. Alas, despite the claim to divine origins, there is no escape from humanity, no way to transcend ourselves: once the word is given, it can be heard and understood only through human ears, thoughts, and understanding.

Believers may choose a particular affiliational or denominational reading of sacred scripture, and delude ourselves into believing that this choice reflects the sole and exclusive meaning of scripture. But a modicum of intellectual honesty is sufficient to undermine this illusion. Regardless of the origin of scripture, there is no escape from human interpretation and application, or from taking responsibility for the choices we make about when and how to apply the "objective" word of God.

Whether divinely ordained or human-based, moral knowledge ultimately ends up in the same location, the human being—who is either the original source or the sole interpreter of the content of the moral principles and their application. As J. B. Soloveitchik argues in *Halakhic Man*, recognizing the centrality of humankind in discerning the good is not merely the foundation of "secular" ethics but of religious-based ethics as well, as God counts on the capacity of humanity to understand and apply the divine will.

TO ERR IS HUMAN

Do humans err in our assessment of the good? We certainly do. Does human moral knowledge change over time? Yes, it does. The obligation of the autonomous moral voice is to access the knowledge that we have at any given moment and to challenge our religious systems to comply. As humans, we have the innate ability to attain moral knowledge—albeit within our historical, cultural, and social sensibilities. While this knowledge is in most cases remarkably consistent, different sensibilities may, and in fact will, produce different judgments. In the end, to paraphrase the rabbinic statement, a person has access only to that which his or her eyes see. (Midrash Tanhuma, Mishpatim 6) Whether as interpreters of scripture or when speaking in our own voice, we are responsible for knowing only that which we can know. Another generation may move forward or backward; our responsibility is to live in accordance with the best moral dictates to which we have access in our cultural and historical context.

To yearn for knowledge that is and will be immune from such vicissitudes is understandable but simply unattainable for human beings, religious or not. The difference between allowing religion to determine the good and positing the independence of the good lies not in replacing moral certainty with relativism, but in replacing the subjectivism of human interpretation of scripture with the best that the human intellect and conscience can ascertain at any given time. When we choose the latter, we add a layer of protection to our moral universe against the dangers of God Manipulation.

"WHERE WERE YOU WHEN I LAID THE EARTH'S FOUNDATIONS?"

In the previous chapter, I argued that God Intoxication can be overcome by establishing the primacy of the ethical over religious theology and authority. Religion must teach that despite God's transcendence, and all the other philosophical and metaphysical dimensions the God idea implies, love of God may not be permitted to induce the intoxication that blinds religious people to the realities of human dignity and need. To the contrary, love of God must be expressed in our ability to make God's name beloved to others through exemplary moral behavior. Religious thought and practice are evaluated according to ethical standards that stand primary to it, not the other way around.

To combat God Manipulation requires overcoming a different dimension of monotheism's concept of God, one also embedded in the notion of divine transcendence. For a transcendent God would seem to be, by definition, an autonomous

God—independent of the world and any of its forces or rules. A transcendent God is sui generis, a being who sets the rules and is not subject to them. A notion of the good that stands over and above divine transcendence seemingly contradicts this core understanding of the monotheistic God.

This correlation between the power of God in history and the ability and right of God to determine the good is the essence of the argument of the book of Job. When Job questions the legitimacy of his extreme suffering—"Where is the justice I deserve?"—he receives the following prophetic answer:

> Then the Lord replied to Job out of the tempest and said, "Who is this that darkens counsel by words without knowledge? ... Where were you when I laid the earth's foundations? Speak if you have understanding: who laid out its dimension, if you know, and who stretched out its line? Upon what were its foundations laid, and who set its cornerstone? When the morningstars sang together, and all the children of God shouted with joy? And who sealed the sea with doors when it burst forth from the womb; when I enclothed it in a cloud, and swaddled it in dark fog? And set my decree upon it, with bars and doors, and said, 'Come this far, and no further; your proud waves will stop here'? Have you ever commanded the day to break? Have you penetrated to the sources of the sea?" (Job 38:1–12)

The essential feature of the theology of the book of Job is the principle of an infinite gap between humanity and God. The act of creation assumes an omnipotent, omniscient God whose transcendence is reflected not only in power but also in knowledge and wisdom. This conception of God gives rise to a neutralization of human reason: Since I don't understand how God created the world, how can I understand God's plans for history? How can I grasp any of God's calculations? This is the stance that is explicitly encouraged by the God of Job. "Gird your loins like a man. . . . Would you void my judgment? Would you condemn me in order to justify yourself? Do you have an arm as powerful as God, and can you thunder with a voice like His?" (Job 40: 7–8)

In the book of Job, to invoke the Socratic formulation, the good is good because God loves it. God has access to understanding, to a comprehension of the correct order of things, that we simply do not possess. The problem is that once God defines the good, it is brought under the purview of theology, and thus subject to the types of theological manipulations that we have seen redefine the good according to the interests of groups claiming the authority to speak in God's name. The concept of divine transcendence once again leads conceptually (and, all too often, historically) to moral corruption in the name of religious piety.

"NOT BY THE JUDGMENT OF HIS SENSES": HIRSCH'S RELIGIOUS PARADISE

A classic Jewish argument in favor of the position that the ethical must be subservient to religious truth was advanced by the nineteenth-century German rabbinic authority and philosopher Samson Rafael Hirsch in his commentary on the Bible. (Genesis 2:9) The second chapter of the book of Genesis tells of a garden in Eden planted by an all-powerful God to nurture the limited and needy human beings. God fills the garden with everything they might require, and in the center plants a Tree of Knowledge of Good and Evil, commanding them not to eat from it.

The story raises an obvious question: What is the point of this temptation? In a garden defined as having everything human beings need, how does the tree-from-which-they-cannot-eat contribute to the paradise of enveloping divine concern?

Hirsch explains this conundrum by asserting that the tree is neither inherently good nor inherently evil. There are, he argues, no magical qualities to the tree; it is not the case that a person eats from it and miraculously acquires ethical knowledge and understanding. If that were so, he posits, why would eating from it be a sin? The purpose of the tree, rather, is to provoke a critical decision point in human history. The tree is beautiful and tasty . . . so what makes it forbidden? Only one thing: God's command. For Hirsch, there is only one requirement that will allow the earth to be made into a paradise for humanity: to define the good according to God's word.

> There is only one condition for the earth to be able to form a paradise for us, and the condition is this, that we only call that good, which God stamps as good, and bad, which He declares as such. But not that we leave the decision between good and bad to our senses. If we place ourselves under the dictates of our senses, the gates of paradise are closed to us, and only by a long way round can Man regain admittance thereto. Yea, the tree could have been called "Tree of Knowledge of Good and Evil" inasmuch as it was to represent to Man, what good and evil was to be to him, what he was to recognize as good or bad. The tree, as we shall see later, was endowed with every attraction for taste, for the imagination, sight, and reasoning judgment, all one's senses declared it "good," that it should be eaten, and yet God had forbidden it to be eaten, was accordingly designated "bad" for Man. The tree, accordingly, was constantly to remind him of the teaching on which the realization of the whole purity and height of his calling depends. The teaching that, according to the judgment of his bodily senses, his mind and understanding, a thing may appear absolutely good, yea the very best, and still to take it may be contrary to the high calling of man, may still be judged by God as a capital crime. The teaching that Man is to recognize what is good and bad, not by the judgment of his senses or his own mind, but to accept the will of God when it has been revealed to him, and

that he must take such a judgment of God as the one guide he is to follow, if he wishes to fulfill his mission on earth, and remain worthy for the world to be a Paradise for him.

For Hirsch, religious people face a fundamental choice, the same choice Adam and Eve faced at the Tree of Knowledge of Good and Evil. The choice is whether to allow ourselves to create an earthly paradise by accepting God's role as the arbiter of the good.

I would argue that God Manipulation proves Hirsch wrong. The moment we allow God to determine the good not only do we fail to inherit paradise, we also transform this world into an earthly hell. For at that moment we unleash upon human civilization the destructive force of a monotheism that subverts ethical standards and trains people to silence their moral conscience, instead piously acquiescing to immoral dictates in the name of God under the pretense of religious devotion.

FROM DETERMINING THE GOOD TO FULFILLING IT: A COUNTERNARRATIVE OF DIVINE ETHICS

The theology of the subservience of the ethical that we find in the book of Job ("It is good because God loves it"), translated into the modern context by Hirsch, represents a powerful narrative of what it means to live with God—a narrative that, as I suggest, culminates inexorably in divinely sanctioned moral indifference. This narrative, so deeply embedded in monotheistic religion (the molecular scaffolding, as it were, of this expression of its autoimmune condition), can only be redressed through a compelling counternarrative. Such a counternarrative, rather than framing God's transcendent greatness in terms of God's ability to determine the good, frames it instead in terms of God's ultimate and perhaps quintessential affinity with the good.

From this perspective, divine greatness and transcendence are not expressed through God's ability to violate the rules of universal morality but precisely in God's innate predisposition to express and be defined by them. The God who becomes God by identifying the nature of the divine with an independent good is the God who understands that the good is independent of Godself.

To combat God Manipulation, moral good must be seen not only as primary to religious truth but also autonomous from it. Moreover, this independence cannot merely be stated or declared; we must be able to construct a compelling and comprehensive narrative within our traditions that foregrounds it. Samson Rafael Hirsch tells a story and offers a choice. If we want our religious traditions to take a different path, we must pave that path with a story of our own, a narrative that redefines essential concepts of God and religious piety and their relationship to the ethical.

HILLEL'S INNER VOICE

A Jewish narrative of ethical independence must begin with Hillel the Elder, one of the founders of the Jewish oral tradition. We return to the story of the non-Jew who asks Hillel to convert him on the condition that he teach him all the Torah while standing on one foot. "What is hateful to you, do not do unto others," Hillel responds. "The rest is commentary, go and study." In the previous chapter, I explained how this source argues for the primacy of the ethical. Upon further analysis, it yields a potent assertion of the autonomy of the ethical as well.

We have seen that when Hillel was asked to articulate the guiding principle at the tradition's core, he does not quote a verse or commandment. To make the point about the primacy of the ethical, he could have quoted, "Love your neighbor as yourself" (Leviticus 19:18), adding that this is the whole Torah, the rest commentary. Or he might have cited its sister verse,

"Love him [the stranger] as yourself." (Leviticus 19:34) Instead, he chooses a formulation with no biblical precedent. In his attempt to provide the key through which the tradition should be interpreted, he offers an articulation invented by himself, suggesting that Judaism's core religious principle is both simple and universally accessible based on one's internal conscience. See others and respond to their needs, treat them how you would want to be treated if the roles were reversed.

What emerges from this dimension of Hillel's response is the essential independence of the ethical from religious tradition. The good around which we aspire to organize our religious lives is not a principle we learn from the tradition but one rooted in the self-evidence of our moral and rational capacities. Thus, with his "What is hateful unto you . . ." Hillel both assumes and asserts not only the primacy of the ethical but also the knowledge of its essential independence.

ABRAHAM'S ARGUMENT

If Hillel establishes a definitive template for a Jewish narrative of the autonomous good, then its founding archetype can be identified in the voice of Abraham at Sodom. (Genesis 18) The Abraham who chooses not to remain indifferent to the potential suffering of strangers—who, instead, stands and fights for their right to be treated justly—personifies the exemplary moral life of a religious hero. His response exemplifies not only the overriding obligation not to remain indifferent but also the essential independence of the ethical sensibility.

> Will you sweep away the innocent along with the guilty? . . .
> Far be it from you to do such a thing, to slay the righteous
> with the wicked, so that the righteous will be judged as the
> wicked. Far be it from you. Shall the Judge of the whole earth
> not deal justly?" (Genesis 18:23–25)

While there are several important dimensions to Abraham's argument, the most significant for the present discussion is his assumption that a self-evident good exists independent of God's word, which obligates God no less than it obligates humanity. Hearing God's intent for Sodom, Abraham does not merely assume that God is, by definition of being God, enacting a moral good. His response neither presupposes that God is incapable of moral failure nor presumes that God inherently defines the good.

Indeed, he goes even farther. Arguing, "Will the Judge of all the earth not deal justly?" Abraham offers a definition of divine transcendence that does not ascribe to God the power to unilaterally define morality. To the contrary, God's greatness is subject to human evaluation. When you act unjustly, Abraham tells God, your greatness is diminished. You are worthy of being the judge of the whole earth only to the extent that you live up to universal standards of justice.

This voice of Abraham echoes powerfully throughout Jewish tradition. It can be heard, for example, in all its prophetic simplicity, in the way the Talmud understood Shimon ben Shetah's response to his students. (JT Baba Metzia 2:5; see the previous chapter.) When he tells them without hesitation to return the found ruby, ignoring the license provided by the legal precedent that Jewish law does not require him to return it to the original (non-Jewish) owner, later rabbis offer the following succinct explanation: "Do you think Shimon ben Shetah is a barbarian?" It is not the law that determines the good, this comment suggests, but a notion of morality independent of the law, which no legal tradition could conceivably override. His commitment to an autonomous good is emphasized through the use of the term barbarian (*barbarun*), which is not a Jewish term but a Greek one. His moral standards are not determined by Jewish tradition but by a universal, independent concept of the just and right.

"Shall the judge of the whole earth not deal justly?" defines the core of Shimon ben Shetah's moral worldview, and the source of his moral courage. Our tradition may fail, he implicitly declares, in the sense of being subjected to God Manipulation that enables religious theology to eschew Hillel's simple imperative while speaking in God's name. Irrespective of these failings, what is required of religious people is no less than what is required of anyone else: not to lower our eyes like Job, in weary resignation, and say we simply do not understand, but to raise our eyes like Abraham, with fierce moral clarity, and resist. To ask God and to ask our religious leaders: Do you think me a barbarian?

"RATIONAL COMMANDMENTS": LEGISLATING ETHICAL AUTONOMY

The principle of the autonomy of the ethical, canonized in Jewish tradition by figures like Abraham, Hillel, and Shimon ben Shetah, also anchors "beyond the requirement of the law" (*lifnim mi-shurat ha-din*), the Jewish legal tradition discussed in the previous chapter as illustrating the primacy of the ethical. If we follow the theology of Job and Hirsch to its logical conclusion—that human beings are incapable of understanding God's plans, and consequently of constructing a system that follows God's will; that we must therefore nullify our own moral sensibilities—then the category of "beyond" becomes impossible to conceive of, let alone practice.

How can we ever go beyond the requirement of the law if we perceive ourselves to be incapable of making any decision independent of divine guidance, much less placing ourselves in a position to judge God in God's infinite and inscrutable wisdom? Another central voice for this theological paradigm, from the medieval period, is the Spanish philosopher-poet Rabbi Yehuda Halevi. In his philosophical dialogue *The Kuzari* (part 1), Halevi explains that the law is like medicinal herbs, whose effectiveness depends on our using them according to the exact prescription and recipe ordered by God. For human beings to attempt to recombine or use them in our own ways, according to our own

logic, he argues, is no different from children playing at being pharmacists—only using real drugs. To live in accordance
with God's will means that the only valid aspiration is to follow
God's prescription as precisely as possible.

This theology leaves no room for the concept of "beyond
the requirement of the law." Indeed, in this context, the very
notion of "beyond" describes a moment of terrified paralysis.
If Nachmanides is correct that no religious tradition can cover
every situation, that there is a moment in which (a) we do not
know and (b) the law does not speak, then we are lost. How
can I be under an obligation to do something for which there is
no clear tradition, which God did not explicitly tell me to do?
If my internal moral intuition is invalid, on what basis do I decide, and on what basis do I act? Moreover, how can I possibly
make sense of the Talmudic opinion that if I am only following
the law, I am creating a society worthy of destruction? (BT
Baba Metzia 30b; see the previous chapter for full quotation
and discussion.)

As we have seen, Nachmanides argues, "Even where He has
not commanded you, give thought, as well, to do what is good
and right in His eyes, for God loves the good and the right." In
this context, "beyond" is simple: God loves the good because
it is good; use that independent principle to fill in the details
where the law has not yet spoken. Continually construct a new
Torah that is grounded in your autonomous moral conscience,
founded on the obligations that conscience prescribes.

Nachmanides further develops this principle in his explanation of the sin of violence (*hamas*) for which the generation
of Noah was judged. (Genesis 6:13) There he addresses the
question, "How could they have been judged for behavior that
had not been revealed to them as sinful by divine revelation?"
He responds that the prohibition against violence is a "rational
commandment," universally accessible to the human intellect
and thus requiring no prophetic instruction. The generation of

Noah was punished not for failing to live up to a divine commandment but for not following a rational, moral one.

This is a category that would be incoherent for Job, Halevi, and Hirsch, despite the fact that the Talmudic rabbis canonized it as a core *halakhic* concept: "Commandments which, had they not been written in scripture, should by right have been written." (BT Yoma 67b) Here again, scripture does not define the good but reflects a preexisting notion of what it entails. This is the same spirit that guided Maimonides to argue that while the Bible allows the heathen slave to be treated with rigor, it is the quality of piety and wisdom to be merciful—a corrective notion that does not emerge from within the tradition but from a source of autonomous knowledge.

REDEFINING RELIGIOUS PURPOSE

In this context, it might seem reasonable to ask, given the overarching commandment to do the right and the good, and the overriding authority of autonomous human knowledge of the good, what purpose or value does a system of particular commandments serve at all? Why should the ethical commitment of the tradition not be expressed in a general law to simply follow the good?

Following the doctrine of Hillel, the purpose of religious systems, commandments, and laws is not to determine moral good in the first place. Rather, they function to remind us of that which we already know, and their primary role is to condition us to overcome the most significant cause of moral mediocrity, which is not lack of knowledge but weakness of character.

When religion is doing its job, it fills the role of moral mentor, reminding, cajoling, exhorting, and at times threatening its adherents to check their self-interest and become people who see others, who cannot remain indifferent, and who define their religious identities as agents of moral good. But for

religion to fulfill this task, it must redefine both the concept and
the role of God, and thus the susceptibility of its adherents to
manipulate God in ways that eschew moral standards in favor
of self-interest.

"WITH WISDOM AND UNDERSTANDING": SANCTIFYING GOD IN THE EYES OF ORDINARY PEOPLE

This notion of the autonomy of the ethical is further expressed
in the laws concerning the sanctification and nondesecration of
God's name. (BT Yoma 86b; see the previous chapter for quo-
tations and discussion.) The God who wants to enter this world,
but whose presence is affected by human behavior, defines both
sanctification and desecration—acts through which the divine
presence is strengthened or diminished, welcomed into or exiled from human life—not according to the rules revealed and
mandated by God but through the experience and intuition of
everyday human beings.

When the very status of God's relationship to humanity, and
the access of humanity to God, is determined by the perspectives of ordinary people, the power to define what is godly or
not godly shifts decisively. It is no longer within the purview of
religious tradition to make this judgment (for example, the position discussed in the previous chapter from Tractate Berakhot
that defines the desecration of God's name as wearing clothing
of mixed kinds); rather, it is precisely the purview of those who
experience the behavior and witness the character of religious
adherents, in real life and real time.

The sanctification or desecration of God's name thus evinces
a fascinating nuance: on the one hand it calls upon its followers to cultivate a God-centered consciousness, declaring that to
desecrate God's name is the most serious offense a human being could possibly commit. However, the power to determine
whether God is worthy of honor or disrespect is given over to

the average person, based on his or her independent moral as-sessment of how religious people ought to act.

Maimonides employs this principle in *The Guide for the Per-plexed* (Part 3, Chapter 31), arguing that the standard according to which Judaism must be judged is not determined by the tradition itself. "For it says, 'For this is your wisdom and your understanding in the eyes of the peoples, who shall hear all these statutes and say, "Surely this great nation is a wise and under-standing people."' (Deuteronomy 4:6) Thus it states explicitly that even all the statutes [those laws whose meaning is supposed to be hidden] will show to all the nations that they have been given with wisdom and understanding."

Religious discourse, in other words, is not meant to be un-derstood as a private, self-referential system. Rather, it must live up to the standards of the good and the reasonable that stand outside it, continually subjecting itself to the evaluation and approval of "the eyes of the peoples." Only when religious discourse meets this open, independent standard do we sanctify God's name and avoid its desecration.

EMBRACING AN INDEPENDENT MORAL CRITIQUE

To this Hillelian narrative I have been constructing as a remedy to monotheism's autoimmune disease—grounded in Abraham at Sodom; personified by Shimon ben Shetah; founded on the principle of "beyond the requirement of the law"; integral to the definition of the central human spiritual aspiration of sanc-tifying and avoiding the desecration of God's name; starkly op-posed to the closed, self-affirming religious discourse advanced by Yehuda Halevi and Samson Raphael Hirsch; and presup-posed by the book of Job as inherent to the notion of a unified and transcendent God—must be added a final, critical turn.

Let us return to one of the more troubling texts of God Manipulation that we discussed in chapter 2, concerning the disadvantaged status of the idolatrous non-Jew in rabbinic civil law. (BT Baba Kama 37b–38a) As we have seen, according to this ruling Jews have no responsibility for any damage their animals cause to the animals of non-Jews, while non-Jews have maximum responsibility for any such damage to Jewish property. Enlisting the notion of chosenness, the Talmudic rabbis manipulate the authority of God to permit the mistreatment of outsiders based on the claim that God, in retaliation for their putative rejection of divine revelation, has essentially divested them of any claim to property rights and turned their money over to the Jews.

According to this internal Jewish story, the moment they did not fulfill the Seven Commandments of Noah—or, the moment they did not choose to accept the Torah—these idolators became second-class citizens in God's universe. We therefore need not treat them as we would want to be treated, for God does not want us to treat them that way, much less require us to do so. In short, those who believe they are chosen by God determine whom God loves and distribute legal and moral rights and responsibilities accordingly. This discriminatory ruling represents one of the great moral low points of the rabbinic legal tradition.

The editors of the Talmud, however, chose not to end the discussion with these justifications for this legally sanctioned injustice. After presenting the justifications tainted by the moral distortion of God Manipulation, the editors of the Talmud bring the discussion to a close with a provocative, self-critical edge. (BT Baba Kama 38a) They tell the story that the government of Rome had once sent two commissioners to the Sages of Israel with a request to teach them Torah. The sages complied, and the commissioners studied the Torah in its entirety—once, twice, then a third time. Before returning to Rome, however, they left their teachers with a pointed comment. "We have gone carefully through your Torah and found it correct, with the exception of this point"—why, they asked, are Jews exempt from paying damages they cause idolators, while the latter have maximum responsibility for any damage to Jewish property?

Despite having offered what the Talmud posits as a seemingly acceptable justification, the Talmudic editors, through this concluding story, betray a lingering discomfort, basically recognizing that despite their own attempt at legitimizing the inequality, the question still looms over the tradition.

"We will, however," the emissaries conclude, "not report this matter to our government."

These representatives of Rome, outside voices who enter into our community, study our Torah, and find clear evidence of self-interested God Manipulation, ask the same question the Talmud has ostensibly just answered. This suggests that the Talmudic editors, ending the story on this disquieting note, were not satisfied with the previous answers given and found them lacking. They enlist the figures of these Roman representatives to voice a critique, as if to say, "We have allowed ourselves to manipulate God in a way that has corrupted our own moral standards." The nature and source of this critique is essential to its point. The Romans serve as outside critics, whose notion of the good is defined independently of the tradition. And it is here, with this voice of external, independent critique, that the story ends.

By choosing to conclude on this evocative and ambiguous note, the Talmudic editors advance the argument that God Manipulation can be overcome when the tradition opens itself to the standards of outside perspectives. For the tradition to live up to its own moral standard, it must submit itself to an independent critique and take seriously the judgments of those not invested in the self-interested inclinations of its members, and thus immune to the blandishments of God Manipulation. These representatives of Rome, whom the text is careful to honor rather than vilify, are not presented as having a superficial grasp of Jewish law. The repetition used to characterize their study—once, twice, three times—depicts an immersion in, and perhaps even an affinity with, Jewish tradition and the Jewish people. This is confirmed by the loyalty and concern they exhibit to the rabbis by not exposing them to the Roman authorities. Despite having found damning evidence that could have triggered retribution against the Jews, they choose to keep their own counsel and allow this incriminating passage to remain a secret.

These are not portrayed merely as the official voices of Rome but rather as true friends whom the rabbis felt had something critically important to say. As such, they serve as a model for how to heal God Manipulation. Do not cast all external critics as hostile enemies. If you do, you will lose a profound resource for moral self-renewal. To the contrary, actively cultivate the voices and embrace the judgments of outsiders who articulate an independent moral standard.

Like the editors of the Talmud, we must make ourselves into those critics, holding our religious systems accountable to an autonomous, universal moral conscience. And we must do so based on a narrative woven out of the sources of tradition itself. For only when such a narrative prevails—when we understand the tradition as commanding us to do the right and the good not in the name of any legal argumentation or precedent but in the name of a moral standard that obligates equal treatment of others—will we finally inherit a religion with the power to resist the corrupting encroachments of God Manipulation.

CHAPTER FIVE

WHEN SCRIPTURE IS THE PROBLEM

THE PROBLEM OF SCRIPTURE

Up to this point in our exploration, I have unpacked two critical distortions of God's word by its human interpreters. God Manipulation and God Intoxication are ultimately human conditions, processes by which individuals attempting to enter into a relationship with God stray from the moral agendas outlined by their respective religious traditions. They explain religions' moral failings as a function of dynamics that are internal to the lives of religious believers. "Who asked this of you?" (Isaiah 1) echoes the exasperation of many prophets with the persistent inability of their communities to fulfill God's commands. It is a frustration the source of which the biblical God never really seems to understand, rooted in a human tendency to become negatively transformed by the encounter with the divine. Somehow, those who hear the word of God—not only average believers but also the authors of religious tradition, the rabbis, priests, and imams—time and again come to distort it.

But intellectual honesty requires us to acknowledge that the sites of moral failure within monotheistic religions are not all products of human misinterpretation or distortion. Sometimes God's word itself, scripture, praises and commands immoral acts. The God who religiously sanctions any war initiated by the chosen people, for example, is not a figment of misinterpretation. Abraham may have suffered from God Intoxication when he arose early in the morning to offer his son—his only son, his beloved son, Isaac—to God. But what was God suffering from when commanding Abraham to make this horrific offering in the first place? Abraham does not misinterpret the voice he hears commanding him, nor do his descendants who derive inspiration and guidance from these verses. Scripture is filled with moral inadequacies and transgressions. The devil quotes it so freely because it is often all too suited to his purpose.

This problem has led many to either deny the divine origin of scripture or to argue that the whole enterprise of religion is unsalvageable, built on a scriptural foundation shot through with moral rot. The aspiration to build a moral universe, this line of thinking goes, is best served when we free ourselves from revelation's dubious claims and authority. This is a powerful challenge to the validity of the religious enterprise—a challenge that demands and deserves a response. What possible remedy could there be when the moral distortions of religion are found not in the failure to hear our traditions correctly but in the bloodstream of tradition itself, in the numerous instances of immorality recounted and acted out in God's name? It is one thing to say that God obligates ritual worship and moral excellence, but human beings fail to heed the word by giving preference to the former over the latter. It is another thing entirely to recognize that religion's moral inadequacies can be carried not only by the human interpreters of the divine word but also in the words themselves, and by extension, in God.

Having explored what happens to human moral standards when God enters the room, in this chapter we will now turn to the inverse phenomenon: What happens to God's moral standards when human beings enter the room? For beyond the human interpretive distortions of God Intoxication and God

Manipulation, embedded in the nature of scripture itself is another manifestation of religion's autoimmune disorder, another moral distortion: this one affecting God, as a consequence of God's willingness to reveal the divine will to humanity through the medium of scripture. To understand the root of this distortion, we must delve into the nature and role revelatory scripture plays in the divine-human encounter.

WHAT IS SCRIPTURE?

If religious life is what human beings create in response to their encounter with God, then scripture, in the religious imagination, is what God creates (or inspires) in response to the encounter with human beings. Belief in God naturally leads to a yearning for revelation, for when God's presence is felt within the life of the believer, it is invariably accompanied by the desire for ever-deepening intimacy.

One natural formulation of this longing is expressed in the question, what does God want of me? The longing to hear God's word is a manifestation of this drive for knowledge of divine will and the heightened closeness such knowledge affords. The idea of sacred scripture is intimately connected to religious aspiration, and at its core it is an expression of love, commitment, and devotion.

In any relationship, mutual commitment and coexistence require the ability to communicate, and God's relationship with humanity is no different. "God spoke to Moses, saying, 'Speak unto the Children of Israel, and say unto them . . .'" Scripture is ultimately a form of God talking. A good thumbnail definition might be: Scripture is a divine response, in human language, to the deep spiritual yearning of God and humanity to live in relationship with each another.

The prevalence of revelation throughout history suggests its deep roots in the spiritual needs of a broad swathe of humanity.

Each of the monotheistic traditions has produced a sacred canon claiming to manifest God's will, and even presence, through its very words. The words themselves express God's desires and expectations, the conditions for receiving divine grace. Revelation addresses the essential longing for spiritual intimacy, and countless believers past and present have devoted their lives to listening.

This is not to say that a direct experience of divine revelation is necessary for everyone. There are always singular spiritual personalities who are able to live with God on the basis of an ongoing inner revelatory experience. Immersed in an unmediated personal dialogue with the divine, these believers rarely experience a lack in their understanding of God's will: what God wants of them is what God communicates to them directly. Grounding both the reality of the divine presence and the contents of divine will in an immediate relationship with God, this rare believer has little need for sacred scripture.

Abraham, one of Judaism's paradigmatic singular believers, possessed no scripture. He lived with God, and knew what God wanted from him through direct revelation: "Go forth from your native land, and from your father's house, to the land that I will show you" (Genesis 12:1); "You shall circumcise the flesh of your foreskin" (Genesis 17:11); and "Take your son, your favored one, Isaac, whom you love, and offer him there as a burnt offering." (Genesis 22:2) He is an individual whose singular inner capacity and drive is to live in the presence of the divine; to walk not only with but "in front of" God. (Genesis 17:1) For such singular believers, compelled internally to construct every dimension of their lives around a covenantal relationship with God, sacred scripture may not only be unnecessary but at times an impediment on their religious path.

For the vast majority of believers, however, this experience of being in a sustained dialogue with the divine is unattainable. They do not hear the word of God being communicated to them individually or directly. It is for such people—the "average believer," who possesses a sincere yearning to live with God as an integral part of his or her life, to hear and heed God's will—that sacred scripture becomes essential. It is through the medium of sacred scripture that God's will—not presence, but will—is revealed. An experience of the divine presence does not require scripture, as nature and human life often hold compelling revelations of their own. But the desire for knowledge of God's will, as applied to the variety of contexts believers face over the span of their lives, necessitates the revelation of scripture.

Those who denounce scripture as no more than a tool for controlling the ignorant—or an escape for the frightened masses seeking to liberate themselves from the bonds of free choice and critical thought, abnegating responsibility for their choices and actions to religion's cynical priests—invariably miss this critical insight about its ultimate source. The inner religious impulse for revelation has nothing to do with human inadequacy or fear. It is a natural consequence of the desire to enter into a relationship with God.

THE NEED FOR SINGULARITY

The moral flaws embedded in sacred scripture can be traced directly to its central mission: to communicate the will of God to the average religious believer. For history has shown that the average believer requires, as a condition of faith in scripture, to locate scripture's origin in a singular moment of revelation, somewhere in the distant past, fixed in time, and closed to further revelatory input. If scripture were constantly being updated by an ongoing and invariably changing set of revelations, how could it provide average believers with the window into the hidden will of God they so long for? Given that ongoing revelation inevitably adds more and at times contradictory messages, how can we ever feel competent to judge what God wants from us?

It is important here to remember the differing religious experiences the singular individual and the average religious person have when encountering revelation. God could reveal to Abraham that Isaac would be his progeny and the foundation of a great future nation constituted by his descendants. But in another moment, the divine will could obligate him to offer Isaac as a sacrifice on a mountaintop altar. If the same voice then declares, "Do not touch the child," that is simply a further revelation of God's will at that moment.

For the exceptional believer, conversations with God are dynamic and can fluctuate in their content from experience to experience. The authenticity of revelation is not judged by the exceptional individual on the basis of its content but by the authenticity the believer experiences at the revelatory moment. As a result, Abraham has no doubt that God wants him to kill Isaac; a moment later, he has no doubt that the divine will is for his son to be spared. In each moment of his covenantal partnership, Abraham simply follows the voice as he hears it, when he hears it. He does not experience contradiction, because he is not interpreting God's will over time but living it moment by moment.

For the ordinary believer, however, there is no such experiential immediacy of the revelatory moment, and consequently, there are no tools with which to measure the relative authenticity of one revelation over another. Abraham experiences multiple, seemingly contradictory revelations over the course of his biblical life. Yet these are all collected and integrated into one scripture. But imagine if the episodes of his story had appeared in different, separate scriptures. What if a scripture were given, for example, which told that Isaac was promised to be the founding father of a nation after Abraham? Then, sometime later, a new scripture, claiming to supersede the first, related that he was instead bound by Abraham at the top of a mountain and sacrificed as an offering to God? And then a third was revealed with the new twist that he was in fact miraculously spared death? How could the average believer judge which of these separate scriptures represents the most authentic expression of God's will? An ever-evolving sacred scripture is counterproductive to the idea of scripture itself, for instead of providing insight into the will of God, it makes such an insight impossible.

It is not that believers cannot handle ambiguity or uncertainty in our religious lives. Every sacred scripture is filled with inconsistencies and contradictions that force the individual to make choices. Scripture itself is never monolithic or completely coherent, and the task of building a religious life entails giving greater weight to certain sections over others, at times consciously or subconsciously choosing to ignore some stretches of sacred text. In our desire to understand the will of God, the construction of coherency through interpretation and selection are inevitable and necessary.

Because of the singularity of scripture, however, this process involves selecting between two ideas that emanate equally out of the same authentic source—neither idea undermining the status of the other as a part of sacred scripture but merely questioning its meaning. Were the inconsistencies and contradictions to be found in different scriptures, however, the debate invariably would lead to the questioning of the authenticity of one "sacred" scripture over the other, with the average believer lacking the tools to resolve the question. This is the ultimate source of the need for scriptural singularity.

As average believers, we can navigate the ambiguity of what scripture means, recognizing that uncertainty is an essential component of human experience. But we cannot navigate ambiguity over what constitutes sacred scripture in the first place. We can determine meaning either individually or with the help of religious leaders and a community of faith, interweaving the processes of interpretation, communal consensus, and the verdicts of history to assist in shaping our choices. But adjudicating a competition between equally valid revelations requires an immediacy of prophetic experience to which we have no access. With no basis for arbitrating among competing prophetic claims, we are scripturally lost.

The Jewish tradition establishes the singularity of its own core scripture, the Pentateuch, by attributing it to the prophecy of Moses and instituting Moses as the only prophet with the authority to reveal divine law. Other prophets may arise and communicate God's will in response to particular historical events, but never establish law that is binding on future generations. This prohibition is so unequivocal that it is enough not only to disqualify the self-proclaimed prophet but also to label him a false prophet liable to the death penalty. (Maimonides, *Mishneh Torah*, Hilkhot Yesodei HaTorah 9:1) Moreover, the authenticity of even nonlegal prophecy is judged to the extent that it can be accommodated within the original prophetic-legal code of scripture. It is the need for scriptural singularity that underlies the Talmudic declaration that since the destruction of the First Temple, prophecy was stripped from the prophets and bestowed exclusively upon fools and infants (BT Baba Batra 12b)—delegitimizing the prophetic impulse as an ongoing vehicle for ascertaining the will of God.

A fascinating feature of Judaism, however, is that this limitation is placed exclusively on the prophet and not the rabbi. In fact, the role of rabbi as lawgiver is so central to Judaism's self-understanding that Judaism developed a notion of two Torahs, one prophetic and one rabbinic; one based on the word of God, the other based on the way human beings understood this law and where they believed Judaism must go. The first is called the Written Torah; the second, the Oral Torah.

The ability of Judaism to contain both, without undermining the religious need for sacred scripture, is grounded on the distinction between prophet and rabbi. The authority of the prophet is grounded in the belief that the word the prophets communicate was communicated to them by God. The rabbi, on the other hand, makes no claim to have heard the word of God, and is ultimately judged by the content of his or her words.

The interplay between the two works in the following manner. For example, from Moses I learn the divine commandment to rest on the Sabbath. As a religious person, I believe that resting on the Sabbath is a fulfillment of God's will. Rabbis might offer competing interpretations of what rest means, but this is a debate over the meaning of divine will and not over two different claims as to what God in fact said when commanding us to rest.

The preservation of this balance is what is at stake in the Talmudic story often referenced by its climactic proclamation, "[The Torah] is not in Heaven!" (BT Baba Metzia 59a–b) Standing in opposition to all the other rabbis of his time on a relatively minor issue of ritual purity—and unable to convince his fellow judges on the power of his arguments—Rabbi Eliezer appeals to God to arbitrate the debate. "Whereupon a Heavenly Voice cried out: 'Why do you debate with Rabbi Eliezer, given that the halakhah agrees with him in every instance?'" In other words, he arrogates to himself the experiential authority of a prophet. But Rabbi Joshua, his leading interlocutor, stands up and declares that the Torah is not in heaven. Once the law has been given, it must be argued based on reasoned debate and decided by the will of the majority. Prophetic voices (even those accompanied by a divine seal of approval) must be disregarded and cast out of the discourse.

Ultimately, the danger of Rabbi Eliezer is that he is demanding loyalty to his position on the basis of the immediacy of his revelatory experience, not on the basis of its content. He is dismissed not because the law is monolithic and there can be no debate, but because he is trying to institutionalize ongoing revelation within the legal system, and this is what makes him a threat to Jewish life and tradition. As such, he loses his authority as a rabbi and becomes no more than a false prophet.

It is important to emphasize that the need for scriptural singularity does not mean that scriptural law cannot develop and evolve. What it means is that changes cannot be justified on the basis of a claim of revelation but only as interpretations of the original, singular scriptural revelation. It is ultimately the community of believers that decides, over time, which interpretation gives the best expression of God's will for them.

Born out of the deeply human longing for an ongoing dialogue with the divine will, the average believer nonetheless requires the singling-out of a particular moment in time, a transcendent historical moment in which God's presence and will are revealed to the community of believers. The function of singularity—the belief in this sui generis revelatory moment, whose transcendent status is transferred to its sacred scriptures—is to provide communities and average believers with an anchor-point of conversation with the divine. The challenge of singularity is that, while advantageous and perhaps even necessary from a religious-existential perspective, it also puts scripture on a collision course with moral failure.

THE BACKWARDNESS PROBLEM

As human societies evolve in their interpretation and application of their moral knowledge and intuitions, by definition earlier moments will fail to keep pace with this progress. Our moral intuitions now recognize as self-evident, for example, the values of gender equality, inalienable human rights and freedoms, cross-religious pluralism and tolerance, the equality of humankind independent of race, nationality, or religious belief—applications of our moral principles that were either absent or less central in the past. But since singularity necessarily enshrines a particular historical moment, and the particular scripture it produced, with the sacred aura of the eternal, we will always be left with a scripture that fails to resonate with the best of what we now know and believe. Scripture is necessarily rooted in, and shaped by, a particular historical moment, and this is yet another reason the devil quotes it so readily.

In a certain sense, the experience of a modern person with the singularity of scripture is akin to that of Abraham in Sodom (Genesis 18), but with a critical twist. Abraham, upon encountering a revelation of God's intent that he deems to be morally flawed, turns and challenges God to live up to his (Abraham's) conception of the good. This challenge, however, occurs within the context of immediate and ongoing revelation, which ensures not only direct communication but also an immediate response and resolution. Abraham, who is fearful that God will kill the righteous along with the wicked, is comforted by God that this will not occur. The moral challenge is resolved within the ongoing revelatory experience. We, however, who communicate with God only through sacred scripture, are left with a text that remains the same even after our moral challenge. We may choose to reinterpret it, or to ignore it, but its explicit meaning and its moral inadequacies remain forever within our tradition, low-hanging fruit for either the devil or his minions to use to give religious justification and sanction to that which we now know to be morally inadequate. By looking backward to hear the will of God as expressed in sacred scripture, we are embedding, by definition, a measure of moral backwardness within our religious lives. This is the "backwardness problem" of sacred scripture.

HOW CAN A PERFECT GOD GIVE AN IMPERFECT SCRIPTURE?

How do we relate to a revelation that purports to reveal to humanity the inner will of God, and at the same time entails content that we experience as blatantly immoral and wrong? For some, this challenge can be resolved only by stripping scripture of its sacred status and freeing ourselves of its authoritative claim. But for many monotheistic believers this is not a viable solution. The desire to hear the will of God is a core element of their religious experience, and this is unlikely to change anytime soon. Yet how can we live with scripture while knowing about this flaw embedded not only within its pages but also within its very concept?

The essential challenge we face is that when we speak about sacred scripture, we are presumptively speaking about God. While the singularity of scripture requires moving backward and sanctifying a particular moment, why does this necessarily embed moral flaws within scripture? Why could God not overcome the challenge of backwardness, and place within the sacred scripture ideas and values that embody moral standards that transcend time and are as relevant today as they were at the time of their revelation?

Since revealed law originates in God's will, must it not necessarily reflect an ideal representation of divine values? Independent of whether the good is good because God commands it or vice versa, ultimately, if God commands it, it must be good. Because, whether or not God encompasses the good, God certainly must *know* what is good. It is thus natural to expect that, in light of its source, such a revelation must be unblemished by moral error. In fact, the claim of moral perfection is as much what we mean when we refer to scripture as sacred as the claim of divine authorship itself. Indeed, the claim of divine authorship is less a historical or factual statement than a value statement that affirms the guaranteed quality of scripture's content.

From this perspective, the idea of such a sacred document accommodating even one instance of moral profanity—much less the few that are well known, and the many that are more obscure—seems patently impossible, an oxymoron. To paraphrase Abraham at Sodom, isn't injustice fundamentally incompatible with the concept of divinity? If so, it follows logically that scripture, to the extent that it is sacred, must represent an ideal expression and standard of human moral behavior, and as such must be immune from the devil's manipulations.

But what if it were possible for a perfect God to give an imperfect scripture? What if, upon further consideration, imperfect scripture is the only scripture imaginable?

HUMAN IMPERFECTION AND SCRIPTURE'S LIMITS

Sacred scripture, while purporting to provide for humankind a window into the will of God, at its core is an anthropocentric endeavor. Its aim is theocentric, in the sense that it purports to serve as a foundation for the average believer to live with God. However, by yearning to empower humankind, the core sensibilities of scripture must be anthropocentric, which is to say scripture must be capable of speaking in a language that human beings can understand.

The God who yearns to be in relationship with humankind, and who provides for the average believer a sacred scripture that empowers humankind to enter that relationship, is by definition constrained by the abilities and sensibilities of the human being with whom God is in conversation. The anthropocentric nature of revelation—its intended audience is human beings—requires that it be bounded in a particular place and time and speak the language of the human beings of that culture and era, with all their moral and psychological imperfections.

Scripture is thus inherently constituted as a compromise between divine will and human limitation. In the Jewish tradition, this idea is classically expressed by the Talmudic principle "The Torah spoke in response to [human] evil inclination." (BT Kiddushin 21b) The unique nature of the revelatory moment—be it during the life of Moses, Jesus, or Muhammad—is thus by definition not a pure expression of God's will. Instead, it must be viewed as an expression of God's will filtered through the mindset and mores of its intended audience. Since the purpose of revelation is to communicate that will to a human audience, its content must be refracted through the lens of what that audience can understand at that time.

This insight plays a central role in the thinking and writing of one of Judaism's most significant religious leaders, Maimonides. In one of his best-known arguments, Maimonides (*Guide* 3:32) asserts that human nature prevents people from moving quickly from one extreme to the other—for example, to abandon overnight all that is familiar and assumed to be true. Human beings do progress, Maimonides explains, but only gradually. Consequently, in his exposition of the sacrificial system outlined in the Bible, a set of rituals designed to create a channel of communication between human beings and God through the offering of animal sacrifices, Maimonides explains that for the Exodus generation, who received the Bible after centuries of enmeshment and subjugation in Egyptian culture, the idolatrous system of animal sacrifices of their former masters was their only frame of reference for communication with a deity. To such people, the demand to use words instead of cattle in their religious rites would be received as little more than incomprehensible gibberish. And so, Maimonides concludes, God suffers more crass, less ideal forms of worship, while shifting the intention of worship from the idol to the one true God.

More than half of the commandments in biblical scripture pertain directly to the temple sacrificial system. Yet according to Maimonides, they represent a profound and necessary compromise by God in the face of the historical context at the moment of revelation. The attitude that allows for this compromise is pragmatic and pedagogical, treating sacred scripture not as the final word on God's will but the beginning of a process of collective spiritual evolution. Just as it cannot be expected of Jews in the thirteenth century BCE to transcend their historical context in the areas of worship, so too would it be impossible to expect the same individuals in the thirteenth century BCE to transcend their current application of the value of equality and apply it to issues of gender, sexual orientation, and the rights of those with different religious and national affiliations.

Sacred scripture thus embodies an inner paradox. On the one hand, it is the necessary tool to enable an individual to know the will of God. On the other hand, it is merely a vehicle to know what the will of God was at a particular moment in time. It provides insight into God's will and, at the same time, into human capacity. For God can only reveal a word in terms that people are capable of hearing and observing.

In a world of moral progress and enlightenment, scripture is at times a beacon of moral greatness—love your neighbor, love the stranger, do not remain indifferent—and at times a mere reflection of the moral mediocrity inherent within a certain social context.

The anthropocentric conception of scripture thus significantly limits the conclusions that can legitimately be drawn about God from its content. In this light, scripture must be assessed morally according to a realistic understanding of its intended audience, and not by the identity of its author.

The act of revelation, then, is not the formulation of an ideal code of behavior but the beginning of a collective process of education. Any good teacher seeks the same elusive balance between meeting students where they are and showing them a vision of what might be. If we view scripture as an educational process, there are profound consequences for how we assess its sacredness and what we can extrapolate from it about ultimate divine values. Instead of judging scripture against our current applications of morality and truth, it should be judged for its pedagogical accomplishments. In this light, taking a primitive idolatrous people and moving them onto a path of incremental moral progress could be viewed very credibly as a success.

Maimonides expands on the pedagogical model of revelation by relating it to the staged process of human development. (*Commentary on the Mishneh, Introduction to Perek Helek*)

In the early phases of education, children are cajoled with crude but effective incentives like honey or sweets. As they get older, the sweets are exchanged for something more abstract—money—and later the money for something more abstract still, the promise of honor. Of course, from the start, the educator's ultimate goal is to instill the value of learning for its own sake. But cultivating this level of consciousness is an extended process of multiple stages.

Similarly, scripture is not intended to reflect the perfect will of God but the stage of human development at which it was given. It offers a revealing window not into the ultimate depths of divine desire but a far more pragmatic calculation about what people in a particular historical era, with all their imperfections, are capable of hearing and doing. It represents an answer to the divine question, how far can I push—what can I demand and obligate—to move the people forward, without creating a system so sacred and pure that it is irrelevant? And it is the task of believers and religious leaders to emulate God with an approach to scripture that continually asks this question anew.

This understanding of scripture creates a space in which the image of God remains intact—with the critical caveat that even the most perfect God cannot give a perfect Torah to an imperfect people. This is not a flaw in God, or even, necessarily, a flaw in human beings, but a flaw in the idea of revealed scripture itself. When the devil quotes scripture, he is often exploiting this flaw. But as we now understand, even when he quotes it word for word, by definition he is taking it out of context, and not, as he would have us believe, merely reciting the transcript of a perfect divine will.

THE ANXIETY OF IMPERFECT SCRIPTURE

If sacred scripture is God's attempt to serve the religious needs of humankind, isn't the idea of an imperfect scripture akin to an operation that is technically successful, but after which the patient dies? God's image is indeed protected from the implications of scripture's moral failings, but where does that leave the average person of faith? Can the idea of imperfect revelation sustain a religious life? Those who look to sacred scripture for guidance in how to live according to God's will would naturally feel this enterprise to be undermined by the awareness that whole swathes of sacred text represent flawed remnants of earlier stages of human moral development. The prospect of acknowledging that while one can be brought closer to God by scripture one can also be led astray, provokes profound religious anxiety. To say nothing of the anxiety that may accompany the realization that, if observed by an individual who has already progressed outside its original historical context, following scripture may actually be a sin.

As we saw in chapter 4, according to Maimonides, a person who follows the biblical laws of slavery is neither pious nor wise, and is in fact acting in a way uncharacteristic of a Jew. The consequences of scriptural singularity present a picture of sacred scripture filled with traps and hurdles, with no internal key explaining how we are to navigate them. The Bible offers no clear code as to which stretches of scripture should be carried forward, and which are to be judged morally deficient and left behind.

HILLEL'S KEY: DECODING SCRIPTURE WITH THE INDEPENDENT GOOD

How does one make sense of a sacred scripture in which two commandments lie side by side on the page, but only one reflects the will of God? A path out of this religious quandary once again begins with Hillel's maxim "What is hateful to you, do not do to your neighbor: this is the entire Torah. The rest is commentary, go and learn it." For Hillel's charge is not only, as we saw in chapters 2 and 3, to use the independent good as the standard by which to interpret Jewish law. That same independent good can also serve as the key with which Jewish believers decode sacred scripture itself. Each subsequent generation of believers who take upon themselves to live by the tradition and carry it forward must apply this Hillelian key to their reading of scripture. Only those values and ideals that embody the application of the moral good of their own era and cultural context are assigned the status of the word of God. Those that fall short are shifted to a different category, one of moral compromise that reflects the capacities and needs of a people at a different stage of moral and spiritual evolution. Some values and ideals subsequent generations of believers have outgrown and some were never meant to be implemented in the first place.

This is the essence of the famous rabbinic marginalization of the biblical obligation to kill the child who is termed "the rebellious son." (Deuteronomy 21:18–21) According to the Bible, if a child behaves as a glutton and does not listen to the words of his father or mother, he is branded with this label. The parents are commanded to bring their child, and their complaint, to the elders who sit at the city gate. If the claim is proved to be true, the child is put to death.

The rabbis of the Talmud (BT Sanhedrin 71a) ask what seems to them a self-evident question: What sin has this child committed to warrant the death penalty? This law is incomprehensible and out of character with everything else they know about their tradition. Their resolution is a model of how one can, and indeed must, use the Hillelian key to read scripture: "The laws of the rebellious son were never implemented, nor were they meant to be implemented." They are rather meant to be studied, and their reward lies only in their study, not their application.

For the rabbis, not all verses of scripture are the same. In some cases, when "God spoke to Moses, saying, 'Speak unto the Children of Israel and say unto them,'" God's intent was to reveal the divine will and obligate us into action. In other cases, however, as the rabbis of Tractate Sanhedrin establish, the intent of God's speech act had no such meaning. It was meant neither to inspire action nor to serve as a window to ascertain God's will. The requirement of the rebellious son is morally flawed, and therefore needs to be excised from Judaism's legal system: "The laws of the rebellious son never were, nor were they meant to be implemented." It still, however, is on the books, a part of sacred scripture. As such, the rabbis posit, God's will is simply for one to learn it.

What is the meaning of a biblical commandment that was never meant to be implemented by anyone but simply studied? The rabbis are creating a new commandment, a new challenge of God to humankind: "Learn it, and therein is your reward." I, God, will give you a sacred scripture, to guide you in a life in accordance with my will. That guidance, however, is not meant to free you from the moral responsibility to walk in my ways by doing what is just and right. I love the good because it is good, and it is not good because I love it. Sacred scripture, however, could lull you into forgetting this, as you find religious comfort in passively following the simple and explicit meaning of the text. The sacred scripture I have given to you is, by definition, filled with hurdles, which challenge you to remain forever vigilant as you work to discern which parts obligate you, and which are not worthy of me, nor of you.

Thus scripture may indeed offer humanity an invaluable window into the will of God and a sacred framework for believers who yearn to align their lives with that will. It is critical to acknowledge, however, that the meaning of scripture is never self-evident: it always requires a Hillelian key to guide us and prevent us from being led astray by its historical origins and pedagogical nature. As we progress and evolve, so does the moral standard required of us by the Divine Educator. And since the revelation that births sacred scripture is by definition a one-time occurrence, the path forward is not in heaven but in our own hands.

A DIFFERENT LEAP OF FAITH

This pedagogical conception of scripture entails a significant leap of faith, though of a very different type from that which we religious people are used to thinking religion requires. For many, the leap of faith into scripture is a leap out of the rational into a consciousness that affirms its inherent, eternal value as a true and perfect transcript of the good, irrespective of what reason might dictate. But the Divine Educator requires a different kind of leap: a leap to believe that wherever scripture contradicts independent moral truth, it does not reflect the will of God; a leap into considering it self-evident that immoral laws were never meant to be applied (if at all) outside a particular timeframe during which people could do no better; a leap into our consciousness that the primary meaning of scripture's divine authorship is that we not allow its moral shortcomings to define our tradition, our God, our communities, or ourselves.

This is a leap that requires us to understand that at times we fulfill the will of God only by going "beyond" the written word of scripture; that reason and morality are not the enemies of God or scripture but the keys to their fullest actualization; that where God is seen as obligating the immoral or irrational, the divine presence among humanity is acutely diminished; that where the tradition is aligned with the best of what we know and believe to be good and true is precisely where religion is most divine.

Again, Maimonides can serve here as our guide. In his discussion of the reasons he rejected the Aristotelian doctrine that the world is eternal—and therefore there was no point at which it was ever created—he makes the surprising claim that his position is not based on the description in the book of Genesis of a world created in time. (*Guide* 2:25) For Maimonides, the simple meaning of scripture is not as the source for knowledge, or even for religious doctrine. Whether the world is eternal or created in time is not to be determined by scripture but by reason. Ever the antiliteralist, he reminds us of the many verses that depict God as having a body, which he, an ardent opponent of anthropomorphism as well, has already reinterpreted or recategorized as allegory.

Thus, for example, when he arrives at the verse in Genesis that describes all human beings as created in the image, or form, of God, with its connotations that ascribe to God and human beings shared physical attributes, Maimonides alters its common reading. (*Guide* 1:1) The thing we share with God, he posits—by virtue of which humanity is said to be in the image of God—is not physical but intellectual, our ability to think and understand. The removal or reinterpretation of these anthropomorphic verses expresses a freedom from the literal meaning of sacred scripture, an interpretive move that is now taken for granted by pious believers, especially after Maimonides. Yet these people of faith rarely admit the larger implications such reinterpretation has on the rest of scripture.

Maimonides does. He argues that the verses establishing the creation by God of the universe in time could have been reinterpreted and allegorized with great ease, indeed far less effort than was needed to eradicate the anthropomorphic vestiges embedded throughout the biblical narrative. For example, Maimonides could have interpreted the first two chapters of Genesis, which describe the process of creation, as an allegory for the purpose of instilling in humankind the virtue of gratitude for the world in which they live, regardless of whether it was actually created by God at a particular moment in time.

"The gates of figurative interpretation are not shut before us," Maimonides announces. If the created-world model were not rational, it would be self-evident that the text does not mean what it seems to, and must be reinterpreted. My acceptance of the creation idea is made possible by the fact that it does not contradict reason and is not intellectually inferior to the Aristotelian option.

For Maimonides, this is the essential leap of faith of the person who believes God commands the good because it is good. These believers never encounter a text that is their master; through interpretation, they are always the final arbiter of its meaning. The unlimited power of the pen of interpretation is not an invitation to heresy but a precious tool for preserving the divine origin of sacred scripture. For God is only God to the extent that God is a God of truth and justice.

Maimonides expands upon this idea when he rejects religious belief that eschews the search for any meaning or reason within Torah. According to this belief, were sacred scripture to be rational or reasonable, it would reflect human authorship, whereas the divinity of scripture is found only in it being irrational, a sign that it could not have been conceived by human beings. (*Guide* 3:31) For Maimonides, those who hold this position possess a sickness of the soul. For they fail to comprehend that God is by definition rational, and ascribing irrationality to God is to diminish God and the religious enterprise, and not to sanctify it. The essence of the divinity of the text is to be located precisely where the text is rational. And so by implication, the more we root out the irrational from scripture through reinterpretation, the more space we make for God in our religious lives.

WHAT'S LEFT OF SCRIPTURE?

At this point it is reasonable to ask, What is left, then, of sacred scripture? If some of it is the domain of the devil, historically relative, flawed and wrong, where can its sacredness be found? And how is it not diminished when we appoint ourselves as the ultimate adjudicators of moral, spiritual, and intellectual truth? If it is sacred only to the extent that it is reinterpreted by human beings, can it maintain a claim to sacredness at all?

The religious pathos provoked by the specter of such questions is what prevents many believers from allowing themselves even to consider the flawed pedagogical model of scripture. But this pathos is founded in a destructive fantasy: the fantasy of certainty. It is a fantasy that sacred scripture is capable of redeeming us from these doubts, that its revelation contains a truth that enables us, with total clarity, to know the good and thus know what God wants from us with the certainty for which we so keenly yearn.

Once we affirm the primacy and autonomy of the good, we are indeed left in a world without recourse to scripture for the arbitration of moral quandaries and conflicts. This may be one implication of the Talmudic dictum "A judge has only what his eyes see." (BT Baba Batra 131a) Our only reliable basis for making moral judgments is the best-reasoned morality of our particular historical moment. Another generation—another person—may disagree. At times the devil may win, and at times the devil may be found in our own faulty logic. But the process of applying humanity's moral evolution to the interpretation and practice of scripture lies at the heart of both the religious journey and the internal culture war that believers must wage if we are to save our traditions from themselves.

The challenge of deepening a religious tradition guided by an autonomous notion of the good forces us to relinquish the fantasy of redemption from uncertainty. But if so, what scriptural stance is to take certainty's place? Is there a form of sacredness that can satisfy the spirit *without* misguided claims of religious certainty?

A DIFFERENT CHOICE

In the introduction I outlined my aim of exposing the false dichotomy between two approaches to religion that I believe are equally destructive and ill-conceived. One remains rigidly committed to the proposition that religious traditions are perfect and that the moral failings of believers are exclusively a byproduct of human weakness. According to this position, the remedy to religion's moral mediocrity is simply to bolster our vigilance in fulfilling scripture's commands. The other approach holds that religion is morality's mortal enemy, that God and tradition do nothing to enhance human moral aspiration and everything to undermine it, and therefore discarding them is a necessary condition for moral progress.

As I have tried to show, many of the moral failings of religious believers can be traced back to the germ cells of religious values and texts. The same sacred scripture that teaches me to love the stranger teaches that the abolishment of slavery is an idea whose time has yet to come. The same scripture that teaches that all human beings are created in the image of God provides an ideological safety net for the self-interests of the chosen.

At the same time, it is a matter of historical record that some of the deepest moral instincts to shape human life and culture over the ages have been cultivated and nurtured by religious traditions and their sacred scriptures. Scripture teaches me that all human beings are created in the image of God, invested with inalienable value irrespective of race, religion, or nationality. And in scripture I learn that being created in the image of God is not merely an honor and a gift but bestows the responsibility to behave ethically and to pursue justice.

It is within my religious tradition that I grapple with the obligation to love my neighbor as myself and to love the stranger and treat the stranger as a citizen. It is a context in which I am constantly reminded that to walk in the world justly is to choose not to remain indifferent to the needs or pain of others; that when someone is in trouble, it is my responsibility to become part of the solution. Religious life is where I enter the sacred time of a calendar designed to reinforce these same values and ideals in symbolic, festive holidays rife with meaningful rituals and spiritual insight. It is where I learn the responsibility and the discipline not only to give lip service to my ethics but also to integrate them into my daily life through rigorous, ongoing self-reflection.

To save religion from itself is to understand that I have a choice—though a different choice, perhaps, than the one I thought I had. It is not a choice between the sanctification of all that is given (despite its corruption) and the rejection of all that is given (despite its profound value). The choice is rather to walk within my tradition, with my God; to hear the word and be inspired and instructed by it; *and,* at all times, to judge it. Sacred scripture is meant to create a relationship between God and humanity, a relationship in which the human partner is inherently challenged simultaneously to learn from, and critique, the divine.

MAKING SCRIPTURE ETERNAL

It is ultimately the responsibility of believers to redeem our scriptures from their historical contexts. The Talmudic story discussed in this chapter, in which Rabbi Joshua defiantly declares to a heavenly voice that the Torah is no longer in heaven, depicts a religious system in which human beings stand as full partners in shaping the future of Jewish life. In this system, God's revealed word is confined to sacred scripture, which relies on human courts and religious leaders for reinterpretation and application according to the needs and sensibilities of each new generation. In the continuation of the story, another rabbi asks Elijah the prophet, the ubiquitous midrashic liaison between divine and human reality, what God's response was in that moment:

"He laughed and said, 'My children have defeated me! My children have defeated me!'"

This pivotal rabbinic moment posits a divine recognition that the Children of Israel are involved in an ongoing process of spiritual and intellectual maturation. The revealed word alone can no longer encompass what we need from sacred scripture: only human hands have the capacity to carry it forward and keep it alive. So God laughs—perhaps ambivalently, but accepting as inevitable this new stage in the covenantal relationship. A possible play on the etymology of the word "defeated me" (Hebrew root, *nun-tzadik-het*)—which in Hebrew is related to the word for "eternity"—suggests an alternate, unequivocally positive gloss on God's proclamation: "My children have made me eternal! My children have made me eternal!" According to this reading, increased human agency and authority as carriers of tradition only enhance God's stature and the sacredness of scripture.

The search for, and the commitment to, the rational is not meant to replace God but rather to serve as the highest expression of love of God. In response to the question, what does it mean to worship God out of love? Maimonides explains that worshiping God out of love is to understand that there are good and evil deeds; that the positive commandments of the Torah obligate the faithful to the good; that the prohibitions are meant to move us away from evil; and that our human essence dictates a commitment to avoiding evil and seeking good. (Introduction to Perek Helek) We love God when we connect to the obligation of completing our human essence and living up to its dictates, and not when we obey God blindly. Maimonides ascribes such blind loyalty to horses and donkeys, who are led to and fro by bit and bridle. It is not worthy for human beings to be led by an external force like this, but rather, he argues, to be guided by an inner sense of what is worthy of the human. It is precisely at this seemingly anthropocentric moment of consciousness that for Maimonides we become lovers of God.

CHAPTER SIX

DO I HAVE TO BELIEVE IN GOD TO BE A GOOD JEW?

GENESIS JUDAISM: IDENTITY AS A BIRTHRIGHT

If one accepts the argument that religion must be saved from itself, and that the way to save it is by putting God second, a natural question arises: Why is God necessary at all? Can I imagine a full, vibrant, meaningful, and righteous Jewish life in which God is not only second but absent altogether? Do I have to believe in God in order to be a good Jew?

To answer this question requires examining its component parts. First, do I have to believe in God in order to be a Jew? Second, do I have to believe in God in order to be good? And finally, do I have to believe in God in order to be a good Jew?

The answer to the first is almost certainly no. A defining feature of the Jewish faith is that it is not primarily a system faith, per se. Jewish identity entails an intricate balance between collective ethnic affiliation and religious practices and beliefs, with the first alone being necessary and sufficient for basic membership. While it certainly includes modalities of action and faith, Judaism is primarily a modality of being and belonging, an ethnic identity with a strong collective consciousness. In the Bible, outsiders could join through marriage, and, since postbiblical times, through conversion. But at its core, to be a Jew is to be born into the Jewish family.

The founder of Judaism and first Jew, Abraham, was a person of faith. The first words of God to Abraham, "Go forth," spark a journey of multiple faith-tests that in turn legitimize his selection as a covenantal partner. However, once Abraham earns this status—whether at the moment he abandons his father's home, his birthplace, to seek the land of Israel; or in his unwavering commitment to God despite a lifelong travail of childlessness; or his commitment to teach his children to walk in the way of the Lord by doing what is just and right; or, finally, his willingness to sacrifice Isaac on the altar of his faith—his descendants inherit this status within the covenant as a perpetual birthright.

> And the Lord said to Abraham, Go forth! . . . And I will make of you a great nation. . . . I will assign this land to your offspring. . . . Raise your eyes and look out, . . . for all the land that you see, I will give it to you and your offspring forever. (Genesis 12:1–2, 7; 13:14–16)

Abraham's descendants warrant God's grace by virtue of genealogy. After passing the daunting test of the *akeidah* (binding of Isaac), in which Abraham is challenged to prove the transcendent exclusivity of his commitment to God, the covenant between God and his descendants is sealed for eternity.

> The angel called forth a second time from heaven, and said . . . because you have done this thing, and have not withheld your son, your only son, that I will bestow My blessing upon you, and make your descendants as numerous as the stars of heaven, and the sands on the sea shore, and your descendants shall seize the gates of their foes. All the nations of the earth shall bless themselves by your descendants, because you have obeyed My command." (Genesis 22:15–18)

They warrant God's blessedness and favor not by virtue of anything they do but simply in consequence of being Abraham's offspring.

This is the essential message of the book of Genesis. As the Bible recounts, neither Isaac, Jacob, nor Jacob's children are individuals of exceptional faith or deeds. Indeed, in many respects they are less than mediocre. The story of Genesis is, in a sense, the opposite of an ancestral hagiography. It is the story of God's steadfast covenantal commitment to remain with the descendants of Abraham in covenantal intimacy amid their toughest travails, wherever history takes them, regardless of—and in many cases, despite—what they do or believe.

This is what I call Genesis Judaism, a Judaism of ethnic identity, of being rather than doing or believing. It is Genesis Judaism that yields the biblical name of the Jewish people, the Children of Israel—a familial term that evolved to encompass a far more complex social structure of belonging, while still retaining its connotations of kinship.

Following this Genesis model of covenantal identity, the redemption from Egypt is not based on the faith or righteousness of the Israelites. God's first revelation to Moses begins,

> I am the God of Abraham, Isaac, and Jacob. . . . I have marked well the outcry of my people that are in Egypt, I am mindful of their suffering before their taskmasters, for I know their pains. And I will come down to deliver them from the hand of the Egyptians, and to bring them up out of that land into a land that is good and large, a land flowing with milk and honey. (Exodus 3:6–9)

The God who redeems is the God of Genesis who has entered into a covenantal partnership with the Jewish people irrespective of what they do, by virtue of Abraham having once walked with God.

EXODUS JUDAISM: IDENTITY EARNED

Genesis Judaism culminated in the liberation from Egypt, and shortly thereafter a new dimension of Jewish identity was revealed. Exodus Judaism, as I call it, introduces the concept of Jewishness as a way of believing and acting. It is in the book of Exodus that the Torah is given to the Jewish people, preceded by this explanation on the foothills of Mount Sinai:

> And Moses went up unto God, and the Lord called to him out of the mountain, saying: "Thus shall thou say to the house of Jacob, and tell the children of Israel: You have seen what I did unto the Egyptians, and how I bore you on eagles' wings, and brought you unto Myself. Now therefore, if you will heed My voice, and keep My covenant, then you shall be My own treasure from among all peoples. For all the earth is Mine; and you shall be unto Me a kingdom of priests, and a holy nation." (Exodus 19:3–6)

The Judaism of the book of Genesis—a Judaism without Torah, without law; a Judaism of core collective identity in which belonging is secured through birth or marriage—is transformed in the book of Exodus into a Judaism of aspiration and obligation. Exodus Judaism is not an identity that is inherited but one that is earned. For it is no longer sufficient for the Children of Israel to be merely the descendants of Abraham, Isaac, and Jacob. Now they must become a holy nation, embracing modalities of doing and striving, not just being. This is not an identity that is guaranteed. To the contrary, it is totally conditional: *If you obey me faithfully, then you shall be my treasured possession.*

After Genesis, the rest of the Torah defines Judaism as an aspirational religion that desires, expects, pushes, and demands the Children of Israel to organize their lives around uncompromising standards of moral and spiritual excellence. The parental

God of the book of Genesis becomes the commanding God of the book of Exodus: "And the Lord spoke to Moses, saying, 'Speak unto the Children of Israel, and say unto them . . .'" This Exodus God will not allow them to rest on the laurels of their ancestors but requires of them to follow an obligatory legal, moral, and spiritual path.

THE GENESIS PREFERENCE: A TRANSCENDENT BOND

Yet despite this dominant sense of Judaism as a religious identity of doing and believing, the central reading within Jewish tradition over the ages is that Exodus Judaism does not supplant or supersede Genesis Judaism. The divine aspiration for humanity, translated into commandment and law, defines the terms of the relationship between God and the Jewish people. But it does not condition, much less compromise, the eternal validity of their covenant: Jewish identity never relinquishes its Genesis mode. As a result, sin, which is an invariable feature of aspirational religion, is not considered grounds for abrogation of the covenant. We may sin, and we may be punished; we may fail, and we may be exiled. But the core relationship of the covenant always remains in place.

> Yet even then when they are in the land of their enemies, I will not reject them, neither will I abhor them, to destroy them utterly, and to break My covenant with them; for I am the Lord their God. But I will for their sakes remember the covenant of their ancestors, whom I brought forth out of the land of Egypt in the sight of the nations, that I might be their God: I am the Lord. (Leviticus 26:44–45)

This principle continues to operate throughout the Bible. This relational bond, the prophets promise, will transcend the exile and bring the Jewish people and God together again.

> But I will not wholly wipe out the House of Jacob, declares the Lord. . . . On that day, I will set up again the fallen booth

of David: I will mend its breaches and set up its ruins anew.
I will build it firm, as in the old days. . . . I will restore my
people Israel . . . I will plant them upon their soil, never to be
uprooted from the soil I have given them, says the Lord your
God. (Amos 9:8–15)

It is also translated into Jewish law as the principle "An Israelite, even though they have sinned, is still an Israelite." (Responsa Rashi 171, 173, 175) Since behavior and belief occupy
a second tier of Jewish identity, sin cannot eradicate the core
covenantal bond. Even a Jew who converts to another religion,
for example, or a convert who immediately recants his or her
conversion, still remains a Jew, according to the dominant position within Jewish tradition. (BT Yevamot 47b)

A sharp illustration of this principle occurred in the case
of a Jewish woman who converted to Christianity in order to
marry an Anglican man. After the dissolution of their marriage,
in 1963 she petitioned the Jerusalem High Court to be allowed
to convert back to Judaism. As the head of court, Rabbi Eliezer
Waldenberg famously rejected her petition. To paraphrase his
remarks: You cannot convert back, because you never left. A
person can no more easily leave Judaism than cease to be the
child of his or her parents. (Responsa Tzitz Eliezer 13:93)

The dichotomy between Genesis Judaism and Exodus Judaism defines even the core of the act of conversion in Jewish tradition. Conversion itself would seem to be possible only
within Exodus Judaism. One should be able to become a Jew
only if being Jewish is a modality of doing, and not exclusively
an ethnic heritage. Nevertheless, the strong imprint of Genesis
Judaism can be found in the way Jewish law defines conversion's
core meaning.

The biblical Ruth, cast by tradition as an archetypal convert,
articulates her desire to join her Jewish mother-in-law, Naomi,
with the following words: "Your people are my people; your

God is my God." To become a Jew, one must affirm both dimensions of identity, the Judaism of Genesis and of Exodus. But the order is significant: first, being and belonging: "Your people are my people"; and only then, believing and doing: "your God is my God." (Ruth 1:16)

Following Ruth, a prospective convert before anything else must first proclaim a willingness simply to be identified as part of the Jewish people—to cast one's lot with this collective destiny, come what may. Only after making a declaration to this effect may the conversion be accepted. Only then is the convert taught the Judaism of Exodus, of believing and doing. As the Talmud proclaims, "A convert who converts is like a baby who is reborn" (BT Yevamot 48b)—reborn, in other words, into the family of Abraham and the covenant of being.

Does one have to believe in God, then, in order to be a Jew? The answer of a Genesis-grounded Jewish identity is clearly and unequivocally no.

This does not mean, of course, that faith in God is not an important element of Jewish religious identity. Indeed, the first of the Ten Commandments is a proclamation of faith, and the next four all relate to the sphere of devotion and action within the Judaism of doing. But the Judaism of Genesis remains as the core foundation of Jewish identity, an identity that cannot be taken away regardless of what one does or believes.

DO I HAVE TO BELIEVE IN GOD TO BE GOOD?

Now let us move to the second aspect of our question: Does one have to believe in God in order to be good? The primary foundation for answering in the affirmative is the notion that only within a relationship with God do I receive God's guidance as to what constitutes the good and am able to act accordingly. A different answer, however, emerges clearly from the previous chapters. If the major trend within Jewish tradition upholds the autonomy of the good from the revealed word of God—grounded not in divine command but moral conscience embedded within the human condition—the answer is, again, an emphatic no. If the good is good independent of God, then the good itself is independent of faith.

The Abraham who declares, "Shall the judge of the whole earth not deal justly?" is attuned to a notion of the good completely independent of God. The rabbinic sage Shimon ben Shetah, who refused to be a barbarian, defines barbaric behavior on the basis of universal moral truths. Hillel, who declares, "What is hateful to you do not to others—this is the whole Torah," has no source within his tradition on which to base this ruling. What he has is a universal truth, which he accesses from within his personal moral conscience.

Does one have to believe in God in order to be good? Certainly not. Indeed, one need only read the daily news to know how commonly belief in God undermines moral behavior. Of course, this is not to say that the two are fundamentally opposed. Belief in God may, in many cases, be conducive to doing the good. It may contribute, through a system of revealed law, to teaching, regulating, and habituating human moral practice. But fulfilling the independent good is, by definition, in no way conditional upon faith.

DO I HAVE TO BELIEVE IN GOD TO BE A GOOD JEW?

The answer to the question, do I have to believe in God to be a good Jew? is more complicated.

The core construct of Jewish identity, as we know, is grounded in the conceptual world of Genesis Judaism. But the evaluative judgment "good Jew" invokes the aspirational language of Exodus Judaism. The question then becomes, what forms of doing or believing, or both, constitute the standard of the "good Jew"? It is at least conceptually possible, certainly, that faith in God is one of them. While basic Jewish identity (or moral goodness) does not require faith, faith may still be a necessary criterion to achieve the fullness of Jewish life.

This seems to be the claim of the Ten Commandments, which might be understood as a biblical articulation of the "good Jew" standard—a standard that includes both principles of faith (the first five) and moral responsibilities (the second five). To the question, do I have to believe in God to be a good Jew? the answer provided by the Ten Commandments would seem to be a clear yes. "I am God," they begin, "who brought you out of the land of Egypt, out of the house of bondage. You shall have no other gods beside me." (Exodus 20:2) Myriad laws that constitute Jewish religious life, guiding our relationships with God and with other people, must be woven together to construct a tapestry of a full Jewish life—the life of a good Jew.

While the answer yes is at least conceptually possible, it is important to remember both Hillel's answer to the convert and its rejection several centuries later by the medieval commentator Rashi (discussed in chapter 2). Hillel was certainly a person of faith and likely had no concept of Jewish life outside a covenant with God. Nevertheless, when pushed to define the essence of Judaism, he defined it exclusively in terms of the aspiration for moral excellence. If "what is hateful to you, do not do to another" is indeed seen as encompassing "the whole Torah," it seems plausible to argue that one can be a good Jew without believing in God.

This stance still does not exclude faith as an important component of Jewish life. But it does mean that moral excellence is sufficient to qualify one as a good Jew. And it is precisely because of this possible reading of Hillel that Rashi felt the need to deny his claim that Judaism's primary concern is with how we treat other people, not how we treat God. Rashi simply could not consider a notion of being a good Jew that does not include the life of faith.

But Hillel's statement stands by itself—and is not as revolutionary as Rashi seemed to take it. Rather, it follows the path forged by the prophets, whose critique against an over-ritualized, morally underachieving people is well known (and outlined in the preceding chapters). And while the prophets did not themselves define Judaism exclusively in terms of the ethical, it is hard to read their words without arriving at the conclusion that what is required of a good Jew is defined primarily in terms of ethical behavior.

> "To what purpose is the multitude of your sacrifices?" says the Lord. . . . "Who asked this of you, to trample My courts? . . . And when ye spread forth your hands, I will hide My eyes from you; and when you multiply your prayers, I will not hear: your hands are full of blood. Wash, purify yourself, put away your evildoings from before My eyes. Cease to do evil, learn well to do good; seek justice, relieve the oppressed, judge for the orphan, plead for the widow." (Isaiah 1:10–17)

This message, echoed repeatedly throughout the prophets, suggests that closeness to God is not contingent on a person's life of faith and ritual adherence but on one's moral commitments and observances. The clear implication of this prophetic argument is that the core definition of what it means to be a good Jew, and the central method of achieving closeness with God, is moral rather than faith based.

In a sense, this conclusion follows logically from my earlier argument about the primacy of the good in Jewish tradition (chapter 3). A system that prioritizes moral goodness over faith and devotion is one that at the very least makes plausible, and indeed seems weighted in favor of, the claim that one does not have to believe in God in order to be a good Jew. As the psalmist declares in the most spiritual and faith-centered of biblical books:

A psalm of David: Lord, who shall sojourn in Your tabernacle? Who will dwell on Your holy mountain? He who lives without blame, who does what is right, and speaks truth in his heart. He who has not slander on his tongue, who has never done harm to his fellow, or born reproach for his acts towards his neighbor. He in whose eyes a vile person is despised, but honors them who fear the Lord. Who stands by his oath, and does not change. He who never lent money at interest, or accepted a bribe against the innocent. He who does these things shall never be shaken. (Psalm 15)

To "sojourn" in God's tent, to ascend the "holy mountain"—this is religious language for being a good Jew. And the standard is moral behavior, not faith.

Do I have to believe in God in order to be a good Jew? I believe the predominant weight of Jewish tradition again inclines toward the negative.

FROM GOD TO GREAT?

While faith in God may not be a necessary condition for acquiring the status of good Jew, and putting God second may be necessary for religion to correct its moral shortcomings, to surmise from this that God has thereby been relegated to insignificance could not be farther from the truth. A core dimension of religious life is its aspirational feature, the demand that we transcend mediocrity, push ourselves beyond what we perceive to be our limits, and strive to reach higher. Religion is one of the central vehicles that can move humanity from good to great. Perhaps I do not have to believe in God in order to be a good Jew. But is faith in God essential in order to be, as it were, a "great" Jew?

It is precisely in the shift from good to great that faith in God becomes more critical to religious life. While not required for a person to be considered a Jew, or even a good Jew, faith is an essential component of Judaism's aspirations for the Jewish people. There is a fundamental difference between asking the question of whether faith in God is necessary and attempting to answer the question of what faith in God does to, and for, a person. While much of this book has been an attempt to diagnose and remedy the moral diseases that faith can produce, my underlying premise is that faith in God should be treated and cured of its pathological side effects so that it can enhance the human condition—not be excised from life altogether.

God enters the discussion in Judaism literally from the beginning: "In the beginning, when God began to create heaven and earth . . ." (Genesis 1:1) But the story of God begins even earlier, with the idea that the God who created the world precedes creation and transcends it. This is the foundational principle of monotheism, which is focused less on the oneness of God than on the quality of God's uniqueness. The God who creates the world, and is not created, is by definition distinct and other from all created beings. As a result, nothing that exists can be associated with God or given divine qualities or standing. The first lesson of the Bible is not that God created the world but that a life of faith is founded on the understanding that we are not God.

As I asserted in chapter 2, a religious consciousness that emphasizes divine transcendence can become a breeding ground for God Intoxication, in which piety is expressed by contempt or indifference toward anything that is not God. God's radical uniqueness depletes ultimate significance from the human sphere, belittling ethics within the context of religious value.

However, God's radical uniqueness can also function in reverse, as the ultimate antidote to human arrogance. As the twentieth century has taught us, some of the greatest evil is perpetrated on others not in the name of a limitless God but on behalf of people and nations afflicted by delusions of grandeur who see themselves, their powers and aspirations, as limitless. The twentieth century has not only taught us the dangers inherent in religion but also the dangers inherent in a world in which human beings perceive themselves as God. This secular arrogance invariably becomes, no less than religion, a foundation for discrimination, racism, oppression, rabid nationalism, and murder, as the world is divided between the elite and the nonelite, the first world and the third, insiders and outsiders, those who count and those who do not. Here, however, it is not God who distinguishes between people but humans, who in their hubristic self-interest allot value to one and insignificance or stigma to others.

I do not want to live with the full self-nullifying implication of the book of Job, but neither do I want to reject its wisdom wholesale. Those who maintain a Job-like awareness that we are "but dust and ashes" may be a little more cautious in their judgments and treatment of others. Faith in God can be the root of the problem, but it can also be part of the solution.

Faith can be a quality that moves a religious person from good to great. For religion can be a system that, while not defining the good, can push, prod, remind, teach, and enable its implementation by addressing our all-too-common deficits, not of knowledge but of inner moral conviction. The challenge we face all too often is our failure to recognize and be formed by the core equality of humankind that is at the heart of Hillel's statement "What is hateful unto you, do not do unto others." Narrow self-interest serves as a foundation for self-delusion and assuming that others are different from me, and consequently may, and perhaps even ought to, be treated differently. The same moral principles that I assume as self-evidently applicable when it comes to my own interests dissipate in the hermetic darkness of human self-absorption.

When the ethical is sought and known on its own terms—when it is both primary to religion and independent of it—then God can enter into human life and become a crucial ally in improving our world. The God who is radically other creates a core equality among all who are not God, a fellowship of those who are but dust and ashes. This equality constrains us to see through our self-aggrandizement, combat indifference toward others in the fellowship, and apply the moral principles that we know all too well.

DIVINE POTENTIAL

The significance of God and faith is not limited to God's potential role in bringing moral goodness to fruition. In the life of the believer, God encompasses the entirety of existence and not only the moral sphere. While remaining cognizant of how the idea of God can serve to undermine ethical life, we must also retain an awareness that this is not the only thing it serves to do. For the religious person, God is both transcendent and immanently ever present—an ideal of radical otherness and holiness and an agent involved in this world, concerned with human behavior, responsive to our needs—and both of these aspects of the divine play key roles in empowering people to live conscious, courageous, meaningful lives.

It is the transcendent God who introduces human consciousness to the experience of transcendence itself. The God who precedes creation reminds human beings that creation, that which is, does not exhaust all that we can or ought to experience. The potential of the religious encounter to touch the holy, to connect to the sublime, to know wonder and amazement, and to move us beyond ourselves and our material existence is a rich spiritual dimension of human life that is cracked open by the belief in divine transcendence. Walking with God is not limited to doing what is just and right, but enables the opening of one's soul to the infinite.

At the same time, God is also immanent. Central to the biblical understanding of the divine is not merely the notion that

God precedes and thus transcends creation but also the idea of God's immense power. The God who creates worlds with a word connotes an almost infinite capacity that stands in stark, daunting contrast to myriad daily reminders of human weakness and limitation. This is an image of a God that rewards and punishes according to human deeds, based on the infinite knowledge, inscrutable wisdom, and ultimate justice, compassion, and goodness of divine providence.

Not-Gods that we are, human beings do not share in God's limitless capabilities. Our ability to control the elements of existence that are most significant for us, most central not just to happiness but also to health and survival, is profoundly limited, threatened, and undermined by the next drought, the next war, the next sickness, the next tragedy, the next accident.

Facing the capricious contingencies built into this-worldly existence is what it means to leave the Garden of Eden. For the garden was a place where we could be human, but without limits. Death was not yet invented, and all that we needed was a hand-stretch away. Yet this limitless existence somehow proved an affront to a core human instinct; while idyllic, we found it far from ideal. Having left Eden, we are now left to contend with the consequences of that choice.

How do I get up in the morning and know that everything that is most important to me might be taken away? That my ability to provide for myself, my loved ones, and my community is highly precarious and in no way guaranteed? And how do I get up the day after a major failure, or after losing someone without whom my life is profoundly incomplete, and continue to live? The valley of the shadow of death is neither a particular place nor an occasional instance but the overarching existential reality of human life. And yet I can walk through it, the psalmist proclaims, "when You are with me"—when accompanied not by the God who plants us in the garden but the God who lives with us in the midst of chaos, who walks alongside us and empowers us to not merely walk through the valley but to build a meaningful life within and despite it.

This aspect of God has proven itself amply vulnerable to corruption and abuse. The God of reward and punishment can become a source of passivity as we wait for divine salvation or a justification for harsh judgments of others in God's name. It may catalyze the misguided zealotry of more than one self-appointed "arm of God," those who are deluded into thinking they are the judges of righteousness and sin, and so dole out reward and punishment accordingly. This God can be a profound source of guilt, self-doubt, and self-criticism.

But the God who accompanies us through the valley of the shadow of death can also be a God who moves and empowers us to find order, meaning, and strength as we make our way through an inscrutable universe. This is the God who is with us the day after we suffer disappointment and tragedy, whose presence comforts and enables us to reenter human life, continually to start over, actively and constructively shaping our own destinies. This is the God whose presence, or indeed absence, is the religiously unanswerable question of the Holocaust. Nevertheless, it was this same God to whom countless victims turned and found the strength to begin again.

"YOU SHALL BE HOLY": THE UNATTAINABLE EDICT

This transcendent-yet-immanent God opens yet another dimension of human potential with the capacity to move the person of faith from good to great. The God who comforts and empowers humanity through its struggles also sets forth the challenge "You shall be holy for I the Lord your God am holy." (Leviticus 19:2) Holiness is not construed by the Bible as a sacred status automatically bestowed upon the Jewish people by virtue of their chosenness. The verse does not say, "You are holy . . . ," but rather, "You shall be holy," setting forth holiness as a commandment that the Jewish people are obligated to strive to fulfill. This commandment to become holy is delivered in a particularly challenging, if not daunting, context: "for I the Lord your God am holy."

It is one thing for scripture to posit a commandment of *imitatio dei* in the context of moral behavior ("Just as God clothed the naked . . . so shall you clothe the naked. Just as God visited the sick . . . so shall you visit the sick." [BT Sotah 14a]). But to be holy, just as God is holy, is another matter entirely. *Holiness,* that most amorphous and elusive religious term, an impressionistic collage of radical otherness, spiritual piety, and exemplary moral character—the closest approximation we dare attempt at describing the divine—seems fundamentally incompatible with humankind. To be commanded to be holy, like God, goes beyond the incompatible to the incomprehensible.

Humankind, inherently and unfathomably distant from the transcendent God, can never mirror, or even approximate, God's holiness. The obligation to be holy because God is holy is in essence a commandment that demands a constant striving for that which cannot be reached. It challenges the Jewish people to never be satisfied with our achievements and never define our ultimate goals in attainable terms. In doing so, it creates a spiritual path that is a perpetual journey of striving to become more. To live with a transcendent God is to acknowledge the infinite gap that exists between us, which has the potential to reinforce the sense of human mediocrity as we despair of ever transcending our original sin. To live with a God, however, who is also sufficiently immanent to command humanity to be holy like God inspires us to believe in ourselves, and it creates the obligation to dedicate our lives to bridging that infinite gap, even though we know it is ultimately impossible. It creates a life of value in the ongoing, lifelong process of striving toward the infinite. "It is not for you to complete the task, but neither are you free to desist from it." (Ethics of the Fathers, 2:16)

THE TARRYING MESSIAH: A LIFE OF ASPIRATION

This charge to live a life of unceasing aspiration is reflected in one of Jewish tradition's rare, popularized principles of faith. From the traditional daily prayer book: "I believe in the coming of the messiah, and even though he will tarry, I still await him, every day, that he will come." The messianic era depicts a time of completion of the human journey through history, beyond which there is no need to improve. Awaiting this messiah can generate a profound sense of passivity, as we anticipate a redemption bestowed upon us by another. In its place, this traditional declaration of faith posits a different model altogether, cultivating the belief not in a messiah who comes but in one who tarries.

The tarrying messiah rejects the notion that history can ever be fulfilled, that human responsibility to complete the task, to continue to strive higher, can ever end. The tarrying messiah posits that any messiah who actually arrives is a false one. In addition, the tarrying messiah does not allow us to lull ourselves into a state of awaiting salvation, to despair from our capacity, and thus responsibility, for improving ourselves and our world. There is no guarantee of redemption in life, and thus no room for passivity or complacency. There is only the aspiration to live in a redeemed world and the consequent obligation to work toward it.

In the life of a religious person, God is a given. But what are the givens about God? One does not have to believe in God to become a good person; one does not have to believe in God in order to be a Jew, nor even a good Jew. God can, however, be a catalyst for doing what is just and right. A life with God can expose humankind to transcendence, opening new religious experiences and spiritual horizons. God can give us the strength to build a life of meaning in the midst of the valley of the shadow of death. God can inspire us to embark on an unending journey of spiritual and moral improvement. A life with God can enhance and deepen the time we are allotted on earth.

Can we be great without God? Possibly. It is clear, however, that we can also be great because of God.

PUTTING GOD FIRST
BY PUTTING GOD SECOND

True humility is not thinking less about yourself,
but thinking of yourself less.
—C. S. Lewis, *Mere Christianity*

TURNING THE SPOTLIGHT ON OURSELVES

I may not have to believe in God in order to be a good Jew, but billions of us, statistically speaking, at least, do choose to make God part of our lives. Good or bad, abstract or immanent, God is with us, and if several millennia of history are any indication, God is likely here to stay. Whether or not God is deemed a delusion is philosophically interesting, but sociopolitically moot with respect to its prospective impact on rooting out the God idea from society at large. For people of faith—for whom belief in God is not based on an argument and thus not subject to being disproved—those who argue God is a delusion are perhaps the most deluded of all.

Nevertheless, it must be acknowledged that both believers and critics bear false witness to not only the content of religious traditions but also the consequences of religious faith. They build worldviews based on lies of omission, and thus trumpet half-truths. Critics selectively blind themselves to monotheism's history as a powerful force commanding humanity to view each other (and ourselves) as divine creations, and thus infinitely valuable. "Whoever sheds human blood, by human shall their blood be shed: for in the image of God has God made humankind." (Genesis 9:6)

Through the lens of the rabbinic tradition, the ethical implication of God's creation of humankind is further elaborated when the rabbis answer this question: Why, as distinct from all other creatures brought into being in the Genesis story, are human beings created in the singular? ("And God said, let us make a human in our image and after our likeness. . . . And God created the human in God's own image" [Genesis 1:26–27]). The rabbinic answer—that those who take a human life, it is as if they destroy the whole world, and those who save a human life, it is as if they have saved the whole world (*Mishneh Sanhedrin* 4:5)—expresses a profound assertion of the infinite value embedded in every human life. The divinity we embody, a transcendent God identifying with finite humanity, which is the engine driving the creation story, is both a cause and an effect of God's profound care and concern for humankind. In turn it obligates religious people, commanded to walk in God's ways, to be caring and concerned for each other. To fail to account for this dimension of religiosity—monotheism's dynamic, indispensable role in elevating moral responsibility throughout human history—is to fail to really see our religious traditions and humanity as it has unfolded and lived with the God idea.

At the same time, religious advocates fail to acknowledge God's undeniable role throughout human history, and into the present, as an animating force for war, murder, and all manner of moral blindness. Our sacred texts, as well as the lived reality of religion and its adherents from time immemorial, are covered in the blood of innocents. To deny that God commands believers to wield the sword in God's name is to ignore the reality of our religious texts and history.

> Then Moses stood up in the gate of the camp and said, "Whoever is for the Lord, come here." And all the sons of Levi gathered themselves together to him. Then he said to them, "Thus says the Lord, the God of Israel: 'Each man strap a sword to his side. Go back and forth through the camp from one end to the other, each killing his brother, neighbor, and kin.'"(Exodus 32:26–27)

The dissonance between religious traditions' contradictory moral voices makes them difficult to contain within the consciousness of a single individual—even though these opposing voices are all contained within the same body of religious thought. For those believers who insist on denying their religion's moral failures, the resolution to this cognitive dissonance is invariably to downplay, deny, or explain away the evil perpetuated throughout their history and embedded in their treasured sacred texts. But the destructive real-world impact of the God who commands evil, and in whose name evil is perpetrated, does not magically evaporate when ignored.

As Justice Louis Brandeis famously remarked, sunlight is the best disinfectant. Religion often seems most comfortable operating behind spotlights used to critique others; religious leaders have a long history of comfortably positioning themselves as social critics of the political and lay leadership of their societies. This is the model embodied by the prophetic tradition of social criticism, of holding a mirror up to society's ethical failings and attempting to project sunlight into the darkness into which our societies and leadership often fall.

But it is time for religion to shine a spotlight on itself, to subject itself to itself—to accountability according to its own standards—and let some sun shine in. Even if God is not a delusion, and if it is simplistic to reduce all evil to a religious source, this should not excuse us from acknowledging that something is clearly broken within our religious traditions.

INSIDER CRITICISM

The courage to see, confront, and not be indifferent to the evil that our religions are capable of perpetrating—the central challenge of social criticism—is only truly effective, as Michael Walzer argues in *Interpretation and Social Criticism*, as an "inside" phenomenon. Effective social critics are always insiders, to some degree, and only by virtue of being viewed as insiders, by other insiders, is there a chance that their words will be heard. Many of religion's most vociferous critics, who see and position themselves as outsiders, do not comprehend how totally irrelevant they are to people of faith. When criticism is offered by one who is not invested in the enterprise, its targets become defensive and dismissive, seeing the criticism not as assistance but as a threat (which is not incorrect). Still, people of faith must realize the indispensable value of receiving criticism, and criticizing ourselves, for the sake of our own communities. We must be, and cultivate, internal critics who can look moral failure squarely in the eye, not as an indictment of religion but as a failure of religion to live up to its own goals.

Here again we need look no farther than the original critic of God, Abraham, and his famous stand at Sodom—a foundational source for the arguments put forth throughout this book.

> Abraham came forth and said, "Will you sweep away the innocent along with the guilty? . . . Far be it from you to do such a thing—to kill the righteous with the wicked, treating the righteous and the wicked alike. Far be it from you! Will not the Judge of all the earth deal justly?" (Genesis 18:23–25)

Abraham did not stand as an outsider, asking God to be someone else; to the contrary, he stood firmly within the tradition he had learned from God, and in that place challenged God to be God. It was you, he said, who taught me that you are the judge of the whole earth, and that I walk in your ways when I do justice and righteousness.

This insider criticism—an argument of internal incoherence, that we are not who we ought to be—is an act of love and of loyalty. Which is why, as in the biblical example in which God "comes down," confides in, and negotiates with Abraham, it is far more likely to be heard.

I titled this book *Putting God Second*, even though I know it is very hard for a person of faith to utter these words, or even—as I discovered when sharing the idea with religious people of different faiths—to hear them spoken. Does this response threaten the ability of this book to fulfill its own criterion of being an "insider" critique that a person of faith is capable of hearing and engaging with? In this concluding chapter I'd like to address both the challenge and the critical necessity of incorporating this concept into our religious lexicons and lives. Ultimately, my claim is that unless we are willing to put God second, we make it impossible for God to fulfill the role in our lives that, according to religion itself, God most yearns to fulfill.

HUMILITY AND THE OTHERNESS OF GOD

Is putting God second a heretical stance? Or is it perhaps nonsensical, because "firstness" is a fundamental and definitional element of the very concept of God? I believe the answer is embedded within an inner tension of religious life and of the God-human encounter.

The beginning of the Bible, "When God began to create heaven and earth . . ." is mistakenly believed to be a lesson about the creation of the world. As discussed in the previous chapter, however, the first lesson of the Bible is neither that, nor how God created the universe. It is that God was not created but rather precedes, and thus exists independent of, creation. With this idea, a core feature of faith is proposed: that to live with God is to live with transcendence, with that which is radically "other" than us and anything we can ever know or understand. Embedded in the Bible's first moment is the teaching that we are not God, and neither we nor anything in the world can ever hold or contain God. To believe otherwise is to remain embedded in the consciousness of idolatry, the antithesis of monotheistic faith.

The religious impact of God's ultimate otherness is the imperative of humility, the recognition that to stand before God requires a posture of profound self-nullification. Abraham's great moment of challenging God at Sodom entails just such a recognition: "Here I am to venture to speak to the Lord, I who am but dust and ashes.'" (Genesis 18:27) This posture is endorsed throughout the Bible. "When I behold your heavens and the work of your fingers, the moon and the stars, which you have set in place—what is mankind that you are mindful of them, human beings that you have taken note?" (Psalm 8:4–5) "True sacrifice to God is a contrite spirit." (Psalm 51:19) "He has shown you, O mortal, what is good. And what the Lord requires of you: Only to do justice and love goodness, and walk humbly before God." (Micah 6:8) "I live in a high and holy place, yet with the contrite and the lonely in spirit." (Isaiah 57:15)

In the rabbinic tradition, humility is defined as the highest of all religious virtues. (BT Avodah Zarah 20b) It defines the core confession a sinner must make when standing before God and praying for atonement on Yom Kippur:

> My God, before I was formed, I was of no worth, and now that I am formed, it is as if I have not been formed. I am dust in my life, how much more in my death. Behold I am before

you like a vessel full of shame and reproach. May it be your will that I sin no more, and what I have sinned wipe away in Your mercy, but not through suffering. (BT Yoma 87b)

The Christian theologian and author C. S. Lewis called pride "the complete anti-God state of mind," a sentiment mirrored in the rabbinic declaration that "he who walks haughtily insults divinity." (BT Berakhot 43b)

For the piously humble, is the idea of putting God second not merely conceptually heretical but religiously incoherent? How could those whose self-image is being "but dust and ashes"— who aspire to internalize a sense of utter selflessness before God—even entertain the audacity to put God second? Everything they believe about God seems to lead them in the opposite direction. The arrogance to stand "over" God that some hear in this formulation seems not merely to challenge but to reject and subvert the core piety demanded by religion and aspired to by a person of faith.

Yet it is also indisputable that this pious humility, which is certainly a legitimate religious value, is the soil that nurtures the autoimmune disease of God Intoxication. Thus those who care about the health of our religious traditions and communities have no choice but to confront it and to ask the fundamental question of what religiously inspired humility really entails— and how it can support, rather than undermine, our deepest moral and spiritual values and aspirations. How essential is seeing oneself as "but dust and ashes," when this consciousness undermines the other goals of religious life? A certain brand of faith undeniably thrives in the midst of self-nullifying humility. But the inability to conceive that God could be anything other than first, that we are anything more than nothing, is what generates the problems of moral failure, blindness, and callousness in the name of God: perennially preventing religion from achieving its mission of moral excellence.

"IN THE IMAGE OF GOD": DIVINE SELF-WORTH

The radical otherness and transcendence of God, grounded in the moment preceding the first verse of Genesis—the basis of the humility that is such a signature of religious piety—is, it must be noted, immediately undermined by the continuation of the story. In the moment that the God who is radically other expresses the will to create, the world that emerges is by definition imbued with profound, divine value. When God ascribes to every phase of creation the attribute "good"—culminating with the climactic stamp of approval: "And God saw all that God created, and it was very good"—it is clearly meant to enshrine in the Bible's readers a sense of reverence and immense value in the physical world.

But the most definitive challenge to a self-perception of radical otherness, and the brand of abject religious humility to which it gives rise, is the doctrine that human beings are created in the image of God. On its face, this simply contradicts the concept of God's radical otherness, as humanity is infused with an element of divinity itself. The full implication of this idea is recognized in the famous rabbinic midrash stating that human beings were exiled from the Garden of Eden because the angels could not distinguish between them and God. (Genesis Rabbah 8:10)

The expression of the godly desire to engage with a radical, nondivine other confers on creation as a whole, and humanity in particular, a status of extreme, if not ultimate, importance. At the very least, it implies a status far greater than "but dust and ashes" and mandates for humanity a sense of self-worth deeply informed by its divine origin.

Being created in the image of God suggests not merely a resemblance and an accompanying sense of inalienable value; what's more, it encapsulates humanity's unique role in the scheme of creation. "And God said, let us make a human in our image, in our likeness, so that he may rule over the fish in the sea and the birds in the sky, over the livestock and all the wild

animals, and over all the creeping things that creep on earth."
(Genesis 1:26) Creation in the divine image is not merely a statement of value but one of purpose: a special charge to humanity
to engage in *tikkun olam*, "repairing the world," grounded in
the responsibility to be God's partner in governing and manag-
ing creation.

Those who are charged to repair the world cannot define the
totality of their psychological disposition in terms of humility.
They cannot see the sum of their existence as being as lowly and
inconsequential as dust and ashes. Abraham, to be sure, recognizing the hutzpah of his intention to bargain with God, uses this
deferential rhetoric to signal respect ("Here I am to venture to
speak to my Lord, I who am but dust and ashes?"). But, lest we
forget, the reality is that he does have the hutzpah: he challenges
God's wisdom, compassion, and judgment and models this con-
frontational posture for his descendants to emulate. In the midst
of a life of deep faith and devotion to God, he is claimed, as an
expression of that faith and devotion, by an obligation to transcend his sense of personal "nothing"-ness and stand forcefully
before God, taking responsibility for his world and demanding
an accounting for the divine plan.

In the biblical story, the recognition of covenantal empowerment that comes with being God's partner on earth is explicitly
recognized, and endorsed, by God. "Now the Lord said, should
I hide from Abraham what I am about to do?" (Genesis 18:17)
God declares that the covenantal partnership with Abraham
entails a vital aspect of human empowerment, which is indeed
required in order to take responsibility for the world we are
charged to settle and preside over.

GOD'S COVENANTAL PARTNER

This idea of human empowerment as the direct implication of
the concept of covenant is the cornerstone of my father David

Hartman's life's work, the central expression of which is his book *A Living Covenant*. As he argues there, it is this sense of empowered self-worth that animates the entire rabbinic enterprise, which sees the word of God as the beginning of a vigorous dialogue with humanity meant to last the span of history. The covenantal system shapes the initial terms of humanity's relationship with God, while creating a space for God's human partners to stand before the divine in their finite personhood and claim broad authority to shape the conditions of the relationship as it evolves through lived experience over time.

"The Torah is not in Heaven!" the Talmudic Rabbi Joshua hauntingly and memorably proclaimed. (BT Baba Metzia 59b) The demand that God desist from intervening in the unfolding discourse of the Jewish legal tradition and allow it to enter into a new era ruled not by prophecy but by reason and intellect—an era in which Jewish practice and tradition become unapologetically "manmade"—is the ultimate expression of humanity's sense of value and empowered self-worth.

Someone who sees himself as dust and ashes, who sees humility as the defining motif of his relationship with God, could never say, "The Torah is not in Heaven." Nor could he imagine, much less emulate, a Jewish leader like Raban Gamaliel. After sanctioning Rabbi Eliezer with a lifetime ban for trying to reclaim prophecy as the ultimate legal authority (only to be rebuffed by Rabbi Joshua's "Not in Heaven" declaration)—and consequently bringing God's destructive wrath down on the world—Raban Gamaliel, the Talmud tells us, found himself (literally) at sea. When God, bent on avenging the aggrieved feelings of the pious Rabbi Eliezer, summoned a huge wave to drown him, Raban Gamaliel "stood on his feet" and declared, "Master of the Universe, it is well known to you that all that I have done was not for my honor, nor for the honor of my father's house, but rather in honor of you, so that disagreement will not multiply in Israel." (BT Baba Metzia 59b)

To argue with God about what God *should* want, to assume that a human being is capable of knowing better than God what is in God's best interest, is the act of an individual fully attuned to his or her immense capacity and self-worth. It emerges from a consciousness of the implications of being created in the image of God and charged with a mission to govern the world.

REDEFINING RELIGIOUS PIETY

And so the God who is not created, and at the same time creates, embodies an essential tension at the core of religious life. On the one hand, God is posited in a position of transcendence against which radical humility is the only possible human response. At the same time, a God who creates and shares divinity with humankind, inviting them into a covenantal partnership with the divine, diminishes that transcendence and requires of this human partner a profound sense of confidence. If the exclusive ideal of religious life were to live in a divinely endowed Garden of Eden in which everything we need is bestowed upon us by grace, then gratitude and humility are the sole defining features that a life with God would seem to require, indeed permit. While most monotheistic faiths include a desire to return to a version of this mythic garden at an unspecified end of days, that is not the reality in which we currently reside. The essence of a life with God is thus to effectuate, through our actions and deeds, as close an approximation as possible to a Garden of Eden in this world. Religious life, then, is both a call to humility and a call to *tikkun olam* by empowered agents fully aware of our responsibility, capacity, and ultimate purpose.

By advancing both sides of the paradox embedded in the idea of a God who is both transcendent and creative, Jewish tradition encourages its followers to hear the call of both—to feel obligated by both—and to strive to assimilate both, simultaneously and somehow in concert. But how? It might be tempting to suggest that the answer is to be found in some form of a balancing act, applying principles of moderation and seeking guidance in attaining a mythic golden mean. I would argue, however, that if the Bible were designed to encourage balance as the resolution to this theological-behavioral dichotomy, the worst way to do so would be to tell two competing, seemingly mutually exclusive narratives.

I believe that faith is less about balance than it is about passion and commitment, and the challenge Jewish tradition poses here is to recognize both humility and empowered self-confidence as essential features of a life with God: to embody each, in its own time and place, as fully as possible.

As discussed previously, pious humility is a primary catalyst for the moral blindness of God Intoxication. Conversely, the religious consciousness of dignity, self-empowerment, and self-assertion—qualities both assumed in and required by any covenantal partner with God—are the psychological foundations of God Manipulation. It is precisely when the idea of being chosen by God meets a human being imbued with self-worth, that the seeds of arrogance, self-aggrandizement, and ultimately moral blindness can flourish. Instead of chosenness being a catalyst to serve God, it co-opts God into the service of humankind. When a self-confident human encounters God, he or she can catalyze the God Manipulation that blinds humanity to the needs of others who they do not believe are as worthy as they to sojourn so close to God.

Both religiously inspired humility and religiously inspired self-regard contain the germs of religion's autoimmune diseases. Completing the paradox, however, is that not only are they the cause—they are also the cure. The moral blindness of the humble believer that is the essence of God Intoxication must be countered precisely by the sense of empowered self-worth that demands human beings be put first. It is the latter that challenges us to live in a dynamic covenantal relationship with God;

to govern and manage the world that God loves; to see God's creatures and care about their needs; and consequently, engage in acts of justice and kindness toward a humanity and world that God values.

Pious humility can mistakenly lead to a life of moral blindness subsumed exclusively by devotion to God—in which that devotion alone is assigned value, and anything and everything else is dismissed as trivial. We need only recall the Talmudic story discussed in chapter 2, in which Shimon Bar Yokhai and his son exit their twelve-month sentence in the cave and begin destroying everyone they see, regular people engaged in this-worldly concerns. God's response—exclaiming, "Have you exited your cave to destroy My world?" and ordering them back into the cave until they can emerge with a deeper appreciation of the value of the created world—reveals that humanity can never only be "but dust and ashes." To be devoted to God without being equally devoted to the humanity that God created, to see God while remaining oblivious and indifferent to the needs of others, is not a paradox but an oxymoron.

Conversely, the sense of spiritual and moral self-worth that comes with embracing the role of covenantal partner with God can generate the delusions of grandeur that are the ground of God Manipulation: the myth that since I alone am truly God's beloved, and God sees only me, I am religiously sanctioned to see only myself. The antidote to this religious narcissism is none other than a consciousness of humility.

How can a human being ever believe that he or she alone is loved by God? How could a particular religion believe that it alone could exhaust the will of the transcendent One? How could human beings ever draft the Radically Other into the service of their individual or national interests? The moral blindness induced by religious solipsism is the antithesis of a life of faith. A religious person may yearn to be chosen, but a humble spirit recognizes that chosenness means accepting a rigorous set of responsibilities, not receiving a surplus of entitlements. We must allow the totality of the idea of a God who precedes creation and the totality of the idea of a God who creates to permeate our imaginations, our values, and our choices.

The power of faith as a force for good can be fulfilled only through an internalization of each of these ideas. The challenge of religious life is to ensure that each serves as the counterpoint and corrective to the other, consistently probing it and holding it to account. Religion will be saved from itself when navigating this tension is an integral part of religious commitment and the life of faith. Religion will be saved from itself, its autoimmune diseases cured once and for all, when we recognize that by putting God second, we put God's will first.

REFERENCES

References other than those below are from the author's translation of the original.

Dawkins, Richard. *The God Delusion*. Boston: Houghton Mifflin, 2008.

Gadamer, Hans-Georg. *Truth and Method*. New York: Continuum, 2004.

Geertz, Clifford. *The Interpretation of Cultures: Selected Essays*. New York: Basic Books, 1973.

Hart, H. L. A. *The Concept of Law*. New York: Oxford University Press, 1997.

Hirsch, Samson Rafael. *Hirsch Commentary on the Torah*. Edited by Isaac Levy. New York: Judaica Press, 1989.

Hitchens, Christopher. *God Is Not Great: How Religion Poisons Everything*. New York: Twelve, 2007.

The Holy Qur'an. Translated by Abdullah Yusuf Ali. Ware, Hertfordshire, UK: Wordsworth Editions, 2001.

The Jewish Bible (the Torah, the Prophets, the Writings): Tanakh: The Holy Scriptures: The New JPS Translation According to the Traditional Hebrew Text. Philadelphia: Jewish Publication Society, 1985.

Levenson, Jon. *The Death and Resurrection of the Beloved Son: The Transformation of Child Sacrifice in Judaism and Christianity*. New Haven, CT: Yale University Press, 1995.

Maimonides. *The Guide for the Perplexed*. Edited and translated by
Shlomo Pines. Chicago: University of Chicago, 1974.

Muslim, Imam ibn al-Ḥajjāj al-Qushayrī. *Sahih Muslim*. Translated by
Abdul Hameed Siddiqui. Delhi: Adam, 1996.

New International Version (NIV) New Testament. Grand Rapids, MI:
Zondervan, 2015.

Sagi, Avi. *Tradition vs. Traditionalism: Contemporary Perspectives in
Jewish Thought*. Amsterdam: Rodopi, 2008.

Soloveitchik, J. B. *Halakhic Man*. Philadelphia: Jewish Publication
Society, 1983.

Strawson, P. F. *Freedom and Resentment and Other Essays*. New
York: Routledge, 2008.

Walzer, Michael. *Interpretation and Social Criticism*. Cambridge, MA:
Harvard University Press, 1993.

———. *Just and Unjust Wars: A Moral Argument with Historical Illus-
trations*. New York: Basic Books, 2006.

———. *Spheres of Justice: A Defense of Pluralism and Equality*. New
York: Basic Books, 1984.

INDEX

Jewish law (*halakhah*): bystander
laws, 31–32; compared to medicinal herbs, 103–4; covenant
with God and, 142; divine
legislation, 27–29; *kilayim*,
49–51, 88; laws of lost property, 29–31, 41, 81–82; laws of
tzedakah (*see tzedakah*, laws
of); limitations of, 76; morality
independent of, 102–3; moral
lapses in, 79–80; portions not
meant to be applied, 128–29;
"rational commandments"
and, 105; Sabbatical Year
(*shmitah*), 35–37
Jewish tradition: act of conversion and, 142–43; autonomy
of good in (*see* ethical autonomy); centrality of ethical in
(*see* ethical behavior); flaws
in, 48, 49, 68, 78–79; humility
in, 162–63; law in, 30–35; primacy of good in, 146–47; sin of
profaning God's name, 83–85,
88; tarrying messiah in, 154
Job, book of, 96–97, 99, 149
Jonah, book of, 26–27
Joshua, Rabbi, 119, 135, 166
Judaism: core religious principle, 78, 100–101; essence of,
55–56, 69–71, 79–80; Exodus
Judaism, 140–41, 144; Genesis
Judaism, 137–39, 144; internal
cultural war, 41–42; as model
of religion's autoimmune disease, 15–17

kilayim, laws of, 49–51, 88

Lebanon War of 1982, 1–3, 58–59
Leviticus, book of, 36–37

lifnim mishurat ha-din. *See*
"beyond the requirement of
the law"
lost property, laws of: "beyond
the requirement of the law,"
81–82; limited to property of
Jews, 41, 63–65; nonindifference and, 29–31

Maccabees, book of, 73
Maimonides, 75; on animal
sacrifice, 124; on creation
of universe, 130–31; on
essence of Judaism, 79–80;
on pedagogical model of
revelation, 125–26; on "the
quality of piety and the way
of wisdom," 77–79, 105,
127; on worshiping God out
of love, 136
mercy: need to strive for, 79–80;
towards slaves, 77–78
Mishneh Torah, 63, 77–78
mitzvot (commandments): laws
of *kilayim*, 49–51, 88; meant
only to be studied, 128–29;
tzedakah, 32–35
monotheism: assigning blame
for failure of, 11–13; critical
flaw in, 13–15; development
of, 3–4; failure to achieve
goals of, 6–11; foundational
principle of, 148; Judaism as
case study of, 15–17; moral
failure of, 44–46, 111–12; notion of divine transcendence,
95–97, 99
moral blindness, 168–70
moral decency, 85, 86–87
moral disagreements, 92–93
moral excellence, 145